MEASURING OCCUPATIONAL INHERITANCE

Progress in
Mathematical Social Sciences

Volume 5

MEASURING OCCUPATIONAL INHERITANCE

THOMAS W. PULLUM

Department of Sociology
University of California, Davis

ELSEVIER

Amsterdam – Oxford – New York 1975

For the U.S.A. and Canada
ELSEVIER SCIENTIFIC PUBLISHING COMPANY, INC.
52 VANDERBILT AVENUE
NEW YORK, NEW YORK 10017

For all other areas
ELSEVIER SCIENTIFIC PUBLISHING COMPANY
335 JAN VAN GALENSTRAAT
P.O. BOX 211, AMSTERDAM, THE NETHERLANDS

Library of Congress Cataloging in Publication Data

Pullum, Thomas W
    Measuring occupational inheritance.

    (Progress in mathematical social sciences ; v. 5)
    Bibliography: p.
    Includes index.
    1. Labor mobility--Mathematical models.
2. Occupational mobility--Mathematical models.
I. Title.
HD5706.P85   331.1'27   74-10262
ISBN 0-444-41260-3

With 15 illustrations and 32 tables

Library of Congress Card Number: 74-10262

ISBN 0-444-41260-3

Printed in the United States of America

Progress in Mathematical Social Sciences

Other books included in this series

Acknowledgements

I wish to thank Morris Janowitz, former Chairman of the Department of Sociology, and Philip Hauser, Director of the Population Research Center, The University of Chicago, for their support and encouragement. They helped make it possible for most of the following work to be done while I was a member of the staff at The University of Chicago.

Above all, I am grateful to my teacher, colleague, and friend, Leo A. Goodman. His contributions to my intellectual and professional growth during the past several years are immeasurable. He has given freely of his time in the preparation of this monograph and, as any reader will observe, most of what follows consists of extensions of his work.

Preface

A variety of specific problems are discussed in this monograph, problems which may at first seem unrelated. This preface and the first chapter will introduce these issues and try to indicate how they relate to a more general theme and to an extensive body of earlier research.

The study of occupational mobility is unquestionably one of the most central areas of modern sociology, a claim that requires no supporting documentation. Prestige and socio-economic status most clearly manifest themselves in occupation in mödern societies, and acts of mobility reveal many of those factors which affect, or are affected by, prestige, status, and occupational membership. Thus one may observe not just that, for example, certain political attitudes are associated with certain prestigious occupations but that, in addition, as a person moves into such an occupational group, his political attitudes may tend to anticipate the change. A number of studies have found that one cannot only predict occupational group membership on the basis of other characteristics of an individual, such as his education, but one can predict *changes* in such membership by including occupation at an earlier time or occupation of father, say.

The basic orientation taken in this book is much different from those studies. First, although data are always collected on individuals as the basic unit, our units of *analysis* will be the occupational group, at the first analytical level, and the collection of such groups, at the second level. We shall conceptualize mobility as movement over persistent categories of occupations. The patterns of movement will define the structure of mobility.

Second, the mobility structure is embedded in a much more

complex structure, which constrains and conditions the patterns of movement. The components of the larger structure are such characteristics as age, sex, mortality, fertility, and economic requirements; these components articulate with the mobility pattern through their joint distribution with occupational group membership.

The underlying objectives are (a) to specify, to some degree at least, *how* these other components regulate mobility, and (b) to discover ways of characterizing occupational movement which is net, so to speak, of the effect of these other components.

The ways in which demographic factors act through the mobility pattern to affect other macro-level variables can be better evaluated once the above objectives have been responded to. For example, it is well-known that in traditional Chinese society, fertility was positively related to socio-economic status, creating a relative surplus of young men from wealthy families. China's detailed inheritance rules, great competition for desired occupations, examination and civil service procedures, etc., were cultural responses to this pattern.

In the West, however, for at least the past few centuries, the relationship between fertility and socio-economic status has been negative, so that in order merely to maintain a static distribution over occupations, recruitment from lower to upper levels has been essential. In such a situation, achieved attributes of individuals may be more likely to dominate ascribed attributes; selecting "in" is different from selecting "out".

For these two contrasted cases, fertility differences by class generate differences in the direction of gross mobility, leading to various cultural mechanisms and, perhaps, influencing ideologies. However, more than superficial analysis requires that, so to speak, we "hold fertility constant", examining the pattern which is residual of the impact of fertility. The present effort does not extend to such analysis, but it should, I believe, facilitate it.

Similarly, we would do well to separate from the mobility pattern the effects of non-uniform occupational distributions and their changes over time. The occupational distribution is viewed herein as a manifestation of the requirements of the economy or technology. There is a lack of precision in this view because supply and demand, at any point in time, are of course not perfectly coordinated. Certainly, as well, the distribution at one point in time constrains the economy and distribution at any later point in time, so that the logical priority, or conditioning effect, is not as clear as in the case of fertility and mobility. But we shall take observed distributions of men as equivalent to distributions of needed jobs, and shall try to "control" for this distribution in various ways.

Supply and demand may be considered as constraints (and, conversely, as predictors) for sub-populations which are homogeneous with respect to some trait, such as direction (upward or downward) of movement. By recombining sub-populations with different parameters for origins and destinations we can improve on the articulation of supply and demand with patterns of movement.

The first chapter will attempt to clarify the concerns raised here by locating them in a body of related research. Chapter 2 provides a format for integrating inter- and intra-generational movement, differential fertility, and mortality. Chapter 3 describes methods for evaluating mobility which is *forced* by differential fertility or by change in group size. These effects can partially cancel or can reinforce each other; in industrial societies they generally reinforce one another to account for a large fraction of gross mobility. In the following chapter a model is proposed to *eliminate* forced movement from a set of data in order to reveal the underlying pattern of exchange between occupational groups. Chapters 5, 6 and 7 concern the development and application of multiplicative models to decompose the mobility pattern. The first of these describes some models in which frequencies are assumed to be the products of a small number of structural parameters. Several summary measures for evaluating the models are developed. They are then, in Chapters 6 and 7, applied to data from the United States, Europe, and some Asian and developing societies. Chapter 8 briefly summarizes our conclusions.

Most readers will find it necessary to have a mathematical and statistical sophistication comparable to that attained in a graduate social statistics course. Most of the technical material which requires more background is located in the appendices.

CONTENTS

CHAPTER 1

Background: models for occupational mobility

1.1 Introduction

The purpose of this chapter is to indicate the range of models for occupational mobility which have been proposed and developed up to the present time. Where specific ideas are introduced that will be developed in some detail later in the present work, mention of later chapters will be made. However, it seems desirable to place these efforts in a unifying structure, and this chapter is an attempt to do that.

A mathematical model is a theoretical framework which can be expressed and elaborated through mathematical techniques. At root it is a set of one or more assumptions. The utility of a model is dependent upon the availability of (1) methods for generating hypotheses from the assumptions, (2) methods for testing these hypotheses, and (3) appropriate data. A useful model in sociology must be capable of expression in terms of sociological concepts and mechanisms. A model is considerably more than an effort to "fit" data (cf. the objectives listed by Herbert Simon (1957, p. 142)).

It is essential to recognize that the structure which a model brings to a sociological problem is more than a null hypothesis. Models also provide bases for comparison, the residual differences from which sometimes form patterns in themselves. The criticism that a model's assumptions are too general is not always in itself a constructive criticism, as detailed assumptions can only evolve from a broader base. But we certainly do not defend the use of assumptions which originate solely in the availability of mathematical methods for handling them, unless these assumptions are subsequently refined.

We may initially classify the modelling of mobility according to two perspectives. Under the first perspective individuals are differentiated by an interval level variable, usually prestige. Multivariate techniques permit incorporation of additional qualitative attributes of the individual and a fairly sophisticated analysis. Svalastoga (1959) and others have used a continuous prestige scale. The present state of the use of the general linear model, particularly, in this area is demonstrated by Blau and Duncan's *American Occupational Structure* (1967).

At the risk of seeming arbitrary, we shall exclude this perspective from this work, referring to it again only at the end of this chapter. The reason for this exclusion is simply that multivariate models for continuous variables are more accessible to sociologists than are the models to be discussed herein, and we believe the latter merit increased attention. The reader who wishes to pursue continuous models is referred to Blau and Duncan and their bibliography.

The second major perspective uses an ordinal or nominal level variable, usually occupational group membership. Again men are the unit of observation. Within this perspective two foci dominate. The first deals with a single pattern of movement (e.g., father's to ego's category). The second focus deals with a sequence of patterns of movement (e.g., grandfather's to father's to ego's category) and the inter-dependencies *between* patterns more than the inter-dependencies *within* specific patterns. The first focus of this perspective will form the major context of this work.

We shall only allude to a third and more recent view, which can be attributed to Harrison White (1970). The "vacancy chains" model is applicable when a job is a "position" which exists whether or not it is occupied. An assignment of a man to a job in a given year indicates that a vacancy (perhaps of zero duration) existed in that job. The man who fills the job has left behind another vacancy, which must be filled, and so on. Conversely, the man who previously held the job reported on will have moved to fill a vacancy elsewhere, etc. Thus each assignment of a man to a job is located on a chain of conceptual vacancies. The chain originates when a new job is created or when a person leaves the system permanently, creating an opening. The chain ends when a job is abolished (e.g., by merger with another job) or when a man enters the system. There is an analogy of this structure of movement within the system and exchange with the outside to Leontiev input-output theory in econometrics (see Kemeny and Snell, 1960, Chapter 7).

2

White develops several sophisticated models along this theme, using a variety of techniques. Unfortunately, few of his results are conclusive, because of his small sample sizes, and it is likely that more straightforward approaches to some of his questions are possible. Beyond this, applicability is limited to only a few man-job systems. However, the concept of the vacancy chain is, so to speak, orthogonal to the concepts of careers of men or of sequences of occupants of a job, and White is able to generate new questions and methods for answering these questions when the model does apply.

We shall attempt to describe briefly and to inter-relate most of the models under the second perspective above. Virtually none of the authors cited have provided the non-mathematical arguments for their models which we feel they require, and we have not the space to supply these arguments here. But we shall try to be explicit about the assumptions that are made and about some of the inferences that are of greatest interest.

1.2 Ordinal or nominal occupational variable: single pattern

Once a number of states have been specified which can be accepted as sufficiently homogeneous internally, the presentation of movement by individuals between states is quite naturally given by a cross-classification table. This table is of a rather special type, however. On the one hand, its row and column categories refer to the same variable, with difference only in reference in time or generation. Consequently the table is square and if, for some reason, we wished to exchange positions of two rows, it would also be necessary to exchange the corresponding two columns. On the other hand, the mobility table does not describe a transaction flow, which also has the preceding properties, for immobility, as well as mobility, is recorded. When the number of categories is small, there may be some unambiguous ordering, e.g., according to prestige, so that ordinal level techniques will be available. With a dozen categories or more, however, there is usually reason to distrust a prestige ranking, and the researcher is limited to nominal level techniques; sometimes the occupational classification does not yield to a substantive ranking even with a small number of categories. It is thus useful to consider models at both the ordinal and nominal level.

To make the discussion more specific, consider the data of

TABLE 1.

Inter-generational occupational mobility in Great Britain, adapted from Glass (see text).

Category of father	Category of Respondent				
	1	2	3	4	5
1	297	92	172	37	26
2	89	110	223	64	32
3	164	185	714	258	189
4	25	40	179	143	71
5	17	32	141	91	106

Table 1, to which we shall refer repeatedly. These data were obtained by David Glass and associates (1954) for Great Britain; adult males were sampled and their own and their fathers' occupations were ascertained. (Our categories 1, 2, 3, 4, 5, correspond to Glass' categories 1–3, 4, 5, 6, 7, respectively.) The first step in an attempt to find a pattern in this table is to standardize (i.e., divide each entry) by the total frequency, 3497, since the pattern is presumably unaffected by the number of respondents in the sample. In this way we obtain Table 2. Denote the proportions in cell (i, j) of Table 2 by p_{ij}, the proportion in row i by $p_{i.}$ and the proportion in column j by $p_{.j}$

The "density" in cell (i, j) can be obtained by a graphical representation in which the proportion of persons in that cell is shown by a three-dimensional block erected on a base which is $p_{.j}$ wide and $p_{i.}$ deep. Let R_{ij} be the height of the block; then $p_{ij} = p_{i.}p_{.j}R_{ij}$ or $R_{ij} = p_{ij} / p_{i.} p_{.j}$. Figure 1 shows these blocks from "above" and labels them with their heights, R_{ij}.

TABLE 2.

Table 1 standardized by total frequency, 3497.

Category of father	Category of Respondent					
	1	2	3	4	5	Total
1	0.0849	0.0263	0.0492	0.0106	0.0074	0.1784
2	0.0255	0.0315	0.0638	0.0183	0.0092	0.1483
3	0.0469	0.0529	0.2042	0.0738	0.0540	0.4318
4	0.0071	0.0114	0.0512	0.0409	0.0203	0.1309
5	0.0049	0.0092	0.0403	0.0260	0.0303	0.1107
Total	0.1693	0.1313	0.4087	0.1696	0.1212	1.0001

Category of Respondent

		1	2	3	4	5	
	1	2.81	1.12	0.67	0.35	.0.34	0.18
	2	1.01	1.62	1.05	0.73	0.51	0.15
Category of father	3	0.64	0.93	1.16	1.01	1.03	0.43
	4	0.32	0.67	0.96	1.84	1.28	0.13
	5	0.26	0.63	0.89	1.39	2.26	0.13
		0.17	0.13	0.41	0.17	0.12	

Fig. 1. Ratios R_{ij} of observed frequencies to frequencies expected under statistical independence of origin and destination in Tables 1 and 2, expressed as heights of uniform-density blocks when viewed from "above".

If Tables 1 and 2 were characterized by statistical independence then each of the R_{ij} would be unity and the collection of blocks in Figure 1 would comprise a unit cube. These heights are the ratios computed by Rogoff (1953), Glass (1954) and Carlsson (1958) in their various cell-by-cell comparisons of observed data with this model of "perfect mobility". Using this model as a standard, we observe from Figure 1 that (1) there is an excess of cases on the main diagonal, and if the classes are ordered along a prestige continuum, then (2) the excess is more pronounced at the upper and lower extremes (a "ceiling" and "floor" effect), and (3) there is a monotonic reduction in the values of R_{ij} as one moves from the diagonal toward the upper right and lower left corners of extreme movement: that is, there is a correspondence between the amount of movement between two categories (relative to the sfandard)

5

and their nearness in prestige. Property (3) is a manifestation of the underlying order of the occupational categories along a continuum — in this case, clearly, a prestige continuum. Except for minor variation, these observations hold for mobility tables from all countries and inclusion of any number of categories. A useful summary measure is the average deviation, in a given table, of R_{ij} from unity. For our data that quantity is 0.43, indicating that the average cell departs in frequency by 43 per cent from the frequency implied by this first standard. Another indicator, the coefficient of dissimilarity (in which the terms in the preceding measure are now weighted by the base areas $p_{i.} p_{.j}$ and the resulting sum is multiplied by ½) is 0.30. That is, if 30 per cent of the respondents in the table of perfect mobility were shifted then the observed table would be achieved; the model correctly locates 70 per cent of all individuals. Considering the simplicity of the assumption, we consider this a good first step.

As Blau and Duncan (1967, p. 93) have shown, this approach does not completely eliminate the effect of the marginals, since by inverting the matrix of the R_{ij} it is easy to reconstruct Table 2. (Strictly speaking, it is possible that the matrix of R_{ij} will not be invertible, but properties (1)–(3) above make this possibility slight.) The model reorganizes Table 2, but does not reduce it in any sense, nor does it remove any effects of non-uniform distributions over categories.

Following this initial grip on the pattern one could proceed in various directions. Strictly in terms of mathematical logic, there are two ways to modify the model of independence without discarding the possibility that the number of persons in a given mobility route (i.e., cell of a table) is proportional to both the origin and destination frequencies. Supply and demand, as measured by the latter frequencies, should and do have major impact, and it is worth trying first only minor modifications of the model of perfect mobility. The first modification is limitation of the model to a subset of mobility routes. This modification, due to White (1963) and Goodman (1965), is referred to as *quasi-perfect mobility*. The second possibility would be incorporation of additional multiplicative factors of proportionality.

First consider quasi-perfect mobility. As mentioned earlier, a table such as Table 1 contains cases of immobility as well as mobility. Blumen, Kogan, and McCarthy (1955) were the first to suggest that these two phenomena be separated (see Section 1.3). Table 1 can be expressed as the sum of two tables, one of which

6

has the frequencies corresponding to immobility replaced by zeroes (the "mover" table), and the other of which has the frequencies corresponding to mobility replaced by zeroes (the "stayer" table). Immobility would first be conceived of as limited to the main diagonal, but could be generalized to include movement between categories which are "near" one another according to an overall ordinal ranking by which the R_{ij} decrease monotonically with movement away from the diagonal (as described above). Under such a pattern of the R_{ij} and with this expanded view of immobility, it is in fact necessary to count as immobile nearly all persons in the upper left and lower right quadrants of the table; at most one occupational group can have non-zero entries in both the upward and downward mobility portions of the "mover" table. (This is indeed a well-motivated implication and not a *post hoc* attempt to improve the fit; for a related discussion, see Goodman (1965), McFarland (1968) and Appendix 4.) Thus as the number of categories increases, the proportion of cells on and near the diagonal which must be allocated to the "stayer" table approaches 0.50.

An alternative decomposition of a mobility table would consider only persons on the main diagonal as stayers, but would subdivide the movers into "upward movers" and "downward movers". Methods for such a tripartite decomposition have been described by Goodman (1968) and will be applied later in this work.

If we follow the model of quasi-independence, which assumes that in the mover table, cell frequencies not constrained to zero are the simple product of an origin effect and a destination effect, then we obtain the ratios R_{ij}^* of the observed values to predicted values given in Table 3. It is clear that for these data, at least,

TABLE 3.

The ratio R_{ij}^* of expected to observed frequency for the quasi-perfect model. Persons in cells marked "−" were considered to be stayers.

Category of father	Category of Respondent				
	1	2	3	4	5
1	−	−	1.04	0.90	0.92
2	−	−	0.99	1.14	0.83
3	1.04	0.94	−	0.99	1.05
4	0.92	1.17	0.98	−	−
5	0.80	1.21	0.99	−	−

the model fits the behavior of the movers quite well. Among the movers, the average departure of R_{ij}^* from unity is only 0.09, and 95 per cent of the movers are correctly classified by this model. When the χ^2 test is applied to the observed and expected frequencies of the movers, we obtain a value of 7.9, with 7 degrees of freedom, indicating that on statistical grounds we certainly cannot reject this model for the movers.

Although the original model of quasi-perfect mobility was applied to movers only, we can also check for quasi-independence in the "stayer" table. Methods described by Goodman (1968) yield the ratios R_{ij}^* for stayers given in Table 4 (one cell has an asterisk because no degrees of freedom were available for its estimation). For the stayers, the pattern of the R_{ij}^* is similar to the pattern of the R_{ij} in Figure 1 and it is clear that the model of quasi-independence does not adequately describe the movement of this sub-population.

If the quasi-perfect model holds for movers, then there is an openness to the occupational class structure to the extent that all persons who have changed class enough to be across the "mover" boundary have overcome any effect of "distance" from their class of origin (at least any effect which can be detected in a crude classification with only five categories). The "movers" are all in the same pool of individuals, their movement governed only by supply and demand, with no remaining impact by differential prestige, etc. Conditions of equal access to skills and positions over all origins would result in perfect mobility. If the bias in such access, which sociological research and theory lead us always to expect, is limited only to certain mobility routes, then a quasi-

TABLE 4.

The ratio R_{ij}^* of expected to observed frequency when the concept of quasi-perfect mobility is applied to stayers rather than movers. Persons in cells marked "−" were considered to be movers. The center cell (marked "*") has no degrees of freedom for a prediction.

Category of father	Category of Respondent				
	1	2	3	4	5
1	1.16	0.69	−	−	−
2	0.68	1.61	−	−	−
3	−	−	*	−	−
4	−	−	−	1.17	0.77
5	−	−	−	0.81	1.25

8

perfect model which "blocks out" these routes will apply. We shall pursue this kind of model in Chapters 5, 6 and 7 of this work.

A second modification of the model of independence would incorporate some indicators of distance between categories; for example, the frequency of cases in mobility route (i, j) could be hypothesized to be inversely proportional to the "distance" from class i to class j. (Social distance is, of course, a concept which has received considerable theoretical and methodological attention. See, for example, Beshers and Laumann (1967) and McFarland and Brown (1971). Goodman (1970) has recently successfully developed a larger class of multiplicative models for mobility tables (and many other kinds of contingency tables). These models develop quantitative forms for status "barriers" and for "inertia".

If one considered the bivariate density of continuous occupational prestige over the unit square with uniform marginals (in effect, "smoothing" Figure 1 to obtain a continuous surface), the result would be approximately a hyperbolic paraboloid (a "saddle"). An adequate conceptualization of the metric and its functional elaboration could be crucial to the value of any mathematical analysis of this density. The reduction of the pattern to a few parameters could permit useful comparisons of patterns from different countries.

Another mode of analysis which, like the above, makes no *a priori* assumption about the ordering of categories, depends on statistical interactions (see Goodman, 1969). Suppose we have a $K \times K$ array of numbers $|a_{ij}|$ which add to zero in each row and each column; if the mobility table is given by the array $|n_{ij}|$ then a quantity of the form $\Sigma_{i,j} a_{ij} \log n_{ij}$ is defined to be an interaction. Subject to the constraints on the arrays $|a_{ij}|$ there will be exactly $(K-1)^2$ such arrays which are linearly independent; on the other hand, there is an infinite number of such collections of arrays, corresponding to different decompositions of the $(K-1)^2$ degrees of freedom of the original $K \times K$ table. Two useful properties, among others, are that (a) the sum of two interactions (or a linear combination of interactions) is an interaction and (b) if the model of independence holds, all interactions will be zero. The estimated variance of an interaction is $\Sigma_{i,j} a_{ii}^2 / n_{ij}$, and if an interaction is divided by its estimated standard deviation it is referred to as a standardized interaction. Interactions are useful in the analysis of any contingency table, since hypotheses about subtables or combinations of subtables can be evaluated. They are particularly applicable to mobility.

The converse of property (a) in the last paragraph is that any interaction, no matter how complex its associated array $|a_{ij}|$, can be expressed as a linear combination of interactions in 2×2 subtables of the main table. Thus if i and i$'$ are two distinct rows, and j and j$'$ are two distinct columns of the main table, then interactions of the form $(+1)\log n_{ij} + (-1)\log n_{ij'} + (-1)\log n_{i'j} + (+1)\log n_{i'j'} = \log(n_{ij}n_{i'j'}/n_{ij'}n_{i'j})$ are the "fundamental" interactions by which it is possible to obtain *any* interaction through linear combinations.

The fundamental interactions with i = j and i$'$= j$'$ can be used to relate pairs of categories. These have the form $d_{ij} = \log(n_{ii}n_{jj}/n_{ij}n_{ji})$, and the special properties (a) $d_{ij} = d_{ji}$ and (b) $d_{ij} = \infty$ if there is not some movement both from i to j and from j to i. As with all interactions, $d_{ij} = 0$ under independence; we know enough of the mobility pattern, however, to be sure that d_{ij} will always be positive. This index can be said to measure the immobility between categories i and j. The $|d_{ij}|$ for Table 1 are given in Table 5, and show a monotonic decrease with movement from the undefined cases i = j, so that the measure is a partial validation of the ranking of the categories and may at first appear to be a distance metric. However, for several cases it happens that d_{ij} is greater than the sum $d_{ik} + d_{kj}$ for a class k ranked between i and j. We thus wish to forestall any interpretation of d_{ij} as a distance metric, but we consider it useful nonetheless.

One can design arrays $|a_{ij}|$ to yield interactions which, rather than relating a pair of categories, instead measure an attribute of a *single* category in a context of several others. One possible array with this use is built up as follows: Consider any fundamental interaction which has i = j, and thus has the form $\log(n_{ii}n_{i'j'}/n_{ij}n_{i'i})$. Such an interaction gives positive weight to persons who inherit category i and negative weight to persons who are mobile

TABLE 5.

Indices of immobility d_{ij} for Table 1.

Category i	Category j			
	1	2	3	4
2	0.602			
3	0.876	0.280		
4	1.662	0.789	0.345	
5	1.852	1.056	0.453	0.370

out of category i (to category j') or are mobile into category i (from category i'). It gives positive weight to the number of persons who move directly from i' to j' in order to balance the role that origin i' has had in the magnitude of $n_{i'i}$ and the role that destination j' has had in the magnitude $n_{ij'}$. Thus this interaction is a partial, positive indicator of the inheritance of category i. It will be zero if simple supply and demand operate within the 2×2 subtable.

A plausible index of the inheritance of i would be the arithmetic average of all distinct interactions of this form with specified i, an index which is itself an interaction. An even preferable index would limit the averaging to subtables which did not include any cells (other than (i, i)) inside an admissible "stayer" blocking, discussed earlier. The index for category 1 of Table 1, under the blocking of Table 3, would be defined by $a_{11} = 1$; $a_{13} = a_{31} = -\frac{1}{2}$; $a_{14} = a_{15} = a_{41} = a_{51} = -\frac{1}{4}$; $a_{34} = a_{35} = a_{43} = a_{53} = \frac{1}{4}$; otherwise, $a_{ij} = 0$. If the implied interaction is divided by its standard deviation, then we obtain a measure which is invariant under multiples of the array $|a_{ij}|$ and has a unit normal sampling distribution under the null hypothesis of independence. The result is the intrinsic status inheritance of category 1, as defined more generally by Goodman (1969).

In Column A of Table 6 we present these measures for all five categories of the British data. The results correspond in their horseshoe pattern with those given by Goodman for a collapsed version of Table 1 and are largely a second manifestation of the horseshoe pattern of the $|R_{ii}|$ of Table 2, with a pronounced "ceiling" and "floor" effect for the ranking used. The negative value for category 3 indicates a relative *dis*inheritance from this

TABLE 6.

Column A: intrinsic status inheritance. Column B: indices of immobility for mover-stayer boundaries of Table 3 (from Goodman, see text). Column C: conditional uncertainty about destination, given origin.

Category	A	B	C
1	17.32	12.00	0.57
2	4.85	2.62	0.62
3	− 1.85	0.68	0.61
4	12.43	3.15	0.60
5	9.91	4.35	0.61

category. Any interpretation of this disinheritance must be tied to an understanding of the basis of the coefficient. For category 3, the total number of persons who have moved to (or from) categories 1 or 2 from (or to) categories 4 or 5 count just as heavily for inheritance as does the number of persons who actually inherit category 3. The fact that there are relatively few persons who make these fairly distant moves gives the measure its low (in fact, negative) value.

Goodman (1969) has also proposed a new index of immobility for category i which is analogous to R_{ii} in that it is the ratio of an observed frequency to a predicted frequency. Specifically, it is the ratio of the observed diagonal frequency to the frequency predicted by the supply and demand effects in the mover portion of Table 3 when extended to the stayer position. This measure is listed in Column B of Table 6 and agrees substantially with the pattern of standardized interactions in Column A. An index of "persistence" of categories has also been suggested by Goodman (1969).

Recently Mosteller (1968) and Levine (1967) have applied to mobility tables a longstanding technique associated with W. Edwards Deming and Frederick Stephan (Deming, 1943, Chapter 7) for the adjustment of table entries to specified marginals in a manner which preserves all interactions (although not *standardized* interactions). Mosteller's motivation was indeed "adjustment" to render tables from different countries, etc., more comparable by giving them the same marginals — typically, uniform marginals. Obviously, comparability of occupational categories is a major requirement if such comparisons are to be worthwhile. Mosteller has found remarkable similarities of patterns for Great Britain and Denmark.

The author has considered an alternative motivation for this technique. Kahl (1957, Chapter 9) argued that mobility has four components: class differential birth and death rates (actually, the role of death rates was overlooked by Kahl), immigration, and change in the occupational distribution — three structural components which "force" an amount of movement — and circulatory mobility. If we conceptualize circulatory mobility not as a residual, as Kahl did, but as the basic pattern of relations between categories, the present object of investigation, which is modified by structural components, then the various models should be compared with a table of circulatory movement, rather than total movement. As a first approximation for recent decades in the U.S.

and other industrial societies we can ignore structural factors other than change of occupational distribution since, as we shall see, this is the dominant factor. We shall also overlook for this presentation the difficulty of overlapping generations described by Duncan (1966). The problem then is to relate the observed table to a "stable" mobility table, representing the circulatory pattern, with the same origin marginals as are found in the observed table but with *the same marginals for destinations as for origins*.

We shall describe in Chapter 4 the justification for interpreting as the "stable" mobility table an adjusted version of Table 2 with destination and origin marginals equal to the origin marginals of Table 2. The circulatory table for Table 2, presented as Table 7, necessarily shows as much total downward movement as total upward movement — that is, the net upward or downward movements of average prestige, etc., for a society are eliminated. There is remarkable similarity, as well, between corresponding frequencies of movement from class i to class j and from j to i.

Kahl (1957) and Matras (1961) added information beyond that which has already been introduced to separate the effects of differential fertility and change in occupational distribution in the amount of mobility each effect "forces", subject to the important assumption that the labor force is replaced by generations, rather than continuously. We feel this kind of analysis is most useful in consideration of a single pattern, although Matras has projected the effects over several generations. Three distributions — that of the labor force at a point in time t_0 (assumed to be the distribution of fathers), that of the labor force at time t_1, and the origin distribution of those persons who are in the labor force at t_1 are compared. The index of dissimilarity computed for the first and

TABLE 7.

The "stable" or circulatory table corresponding to Table 2 (with origin and destination marginals equal to the origin marginals of Table 2).

Category of father	Category of Respondent				
	1	2	3	4	5
1	0.0871	0.0283	0.0491	0.0076	0.0063
2	0.0267	0.0347	0.0652	0.0135	0.0079
3	0.0509	0.0603	0.2158	0.0562	0.0486
4	0.0082	0.0138	0.0570	0.0328	0.0192
5	0.0055	0.0110	0.0448	0.0208	0.0286

third distributions gives the proportional shift from fathers' distribution to the origin distribution of their sons, due entirely to differential fertility. The index computed for the first and second distributions gives the proportional shift from the distribution of the labor forces at t_0 to that at t_1. The index computed for the second and third distributions (the destination and origin distributions of the usual mobility table) gives the net shift from origin to destination due to combined effects. Each of these indices gives the proportion of persons in each case who are "forced" to move. Matras found that for a gross three-way classification in Western countries and Japan, the residual amount of movement is remarkably constant. For U.S. data from Kahl (1957) giving class-specific net reproduction rates for eight occupational groups and $t_0 = 1920$, $t_1 = 1950$, it was found that 23 per cent of the movement in this interval was "forced". These ideas are extended in Chapter 3 herein.

The analysis in the preceding paragraphs is seriously flawed by the concept of the "generation" and the fact that the origin distribution of an inter-generational table does not comprise a distribution of the labor force at any point in time. But we believe this analysis is a good starting point for work which is yet to be done and, taken qualitatively, most of its conclusions are probably valid.

McFarland (1969) has applied the uncertainty function for a set of categories, $H = -\Sigma_i p_i \log p_i$, to mobility tables, using a bivariate form for the function. The base of the logarithms is arbitrary, and since tables for base 10 are more easily found than tables for base 2, which is used in many applications, we shall (with McFarland) use base 10. Uncertainty is a non-negative function which is a maximum ($\log K$, where K is the number of categories) when the probability is uniformly dispersed over all categories, and in this event one will gain the greatest amount of information when the actual outcome is learned. Thus H is also a measure of information. It makes no use of any ordinal property of the variable being considered. McFarland found that H can provide for categorical data an alternative to the product-moment correlation, which requires (as a minimum) continuity. In the context of occupational mobility, the level of uncertainty about destination, given origin, is an indicator of the "permeability" of the occupational structure as it affects the movement of persons in each origin.

14

We have recomputed the conditional uncertainty for each category in the five-category British table (see Column C of Table 6) to permit comparison with the quantities in Columns A and B of Table 6. Although inheritance-immobility and permeability may complement one another according to their dictionary definitions, the measures which have been associated with the concepts are far from complementary. In particular, H does not distinguish between changing category (disinheritance) or being immobile (inheritance); it can only measure departures from a uniform distribution over destinations (given origin). It makes no use of the knowledge that in a mobility table the first row and the first column, say, refer to the same occupational category. Other criticisms are raised by Goodman (1969b). For these reasons the pattern of Column C is unrelated to the patterns of Columns A and B. Note that the uncertainty level is nearly constant over origins. (The maximum uncertainty over five destinations would be 0.70.)

1.3 Ordinal or nominal occupational variable: successive patterns

Much work has been done in this area which exploits powerful statistical methods, in particular Markov processes. Unfortunately, too often the assumptions of the methods are not recognized, and too often only asymptotic results, which are most sensitive to the assumptions, are used. The review of these models will therefore have a critical tone, and will emphasize the recent awareness of the difficulties.

Suppose that we had data concerning occupational group membership for a cohort of men at time t who were, say, age 20 to 24 at last birthday. Of this group, we shall say $n_i(t)$ were in category i at time t. If we followed the movement of those who survived five years, to time $t + 5$, we could readily compute transition rates $p_{ij}(t)$, the proportion of persons in category i at time t who are in category j at time $t + 5$; if $u_i(20)$ is the proportion of persons of age 20–24 in category i who will die in five years then $\Sigma_j p_{ij}(t) = 1 - u_i(20)$ for each origin i. And, by definition of these rates, $n_j(t + 5) = \Sigma_i n_i(t) p_{ij}(t)$ for each destination j. If we have J categories (including the employed and unemployed in each category) this activity can be represented by the matrix equation

$$[n_1(t+5), \ldots, n_K(t+5), d(t+5)]$$

$$
= [n_1(t), \ldots, n_J(t), 0]
\begin{pmatrix}
p_{11}(t) \ldots p_{1J}(t)\, u_1(20) \\
\vdots \qquad \vdots \qquad \vdots \\
\vdots \qquad \vdots \qquad \vdots \\
\vdots \qquad \vdots \qquad \vdots \\
p_{J1}(t) \ldots p_{JJ}(t)\, u_J(20) \\
0 \qquad \ldots 0 \qquad 1
\end{pmatrix}
$$

In abbreviated form, $\tilde{N}(t+5) = \tilde{N}(t)\, \tilde{P}(t, 20)$, where the $\tilde{N}$ are row vectors. The far right entry in the row vector $\tilde{N}(t+5)$ is the number of persons in the original population who have died by time $t + 5$. $\tilde{P}(t, 20)$ is a $(J+1) \times (J+1)$ stochastic matrix (each entry is non-negative and the sum over each of its rows is unity).

The preceding is nothing more than a method for naming some data; it is not in any sense a model, for we have made no assumptions. If we followed the cohort for another five years, with complete data, we could write $\tilde{N}(t+10) = \tilde{N}(t+5)\, \tilde{P}(t+5, 25) = \tilde{N}(t)\, \tilde{P}(t, 20)\, P(t+5, 25)$; we could, theoretically, describe the behavior of the cohort until it became extinct by the effect of a long sequence of transition matrices upon the original distribution vector. We would still not have a model.

We shall describe the assumptions concerning such a process that can be made to "permit" application of the theory of Markov processes. We characteristically have data on only two points in time, say t and $t + 5$, obtained from persons alive at time $t + 5$. If we (1) ignore mortality, in particular age- and origin-specific mortality, then we can incompletely describe the cohort's activities by the equation $N(t+5) = N(t)\, P(t)$. Here $N(t+5)$ and $N(t)$ are row vectors missing the last entry of $\tilde{N}(t+5)$ and $\tilde{N}(t)$, the decedents, and the matrix $P(t)$ is stochastic but is based just upon the surviving population at time $t + 5$. In order to project beyond time $t + 5$ we might assume that (2) all persons in the population are subject to the same set of transition rates during the interval. That is, they are *homogeneous* with respect to characteristics other than occupation (equivalently, occupational movement is determined solely by previous occupation). We might assume (3) the incomplete matrices $P(t)$, $P(t + 5)$, etc., are all equal: the transition matrices are *stationary*. Finally, we might assume that (4) only one's occupation five years previous is relevant to present occupation; there is no carryover effect from earlier categories; this is the *Markovian* (first-order Markovian) property. Then the projection to time $t + 5s$ for integral positive s will be $N(t + 5s) = N(t) P(t)^s$.

The two greatest shortcomings of such an intra-generational projection are the failure to extinguish the population for large s and concealment of the well-known reduction in mobility for older persons. When applied to inter-generational movement, the model (5) ignores differential fertility and (6) assumes instantaneous replacement of one generation by another, rather than a fluid overlap of cohorts. More subtly, perhaps, stationarity ignores the impact of changes in the technology, etc., on the occupational distribution, and (1) and (5) ignore the effect (though slight, in the short run) of a changing age structure on occupational supply and demand. For further discussion, the reader is again referred to Duncan (1966).

Prais (1955) and Blumen, Kogan, and McCarthy (1955) were the first to apply the model of a first-order regular Markov process to mobility — the former to inter-generational movement, the latter to intra-generational movement. The motivation has largely been the convergence of the alleged process to a stable distribution which does not depend on the origin distribution (see Kemeny and Snell, 1960, Chapter 4). As in stable population theory, this distribution should be viewed as a characterization or summary of the present rates rather than as a prediction; even so, the assumptions, particularly the Markov assumption, are more difficult to defend than in mathematical demography. Matras (1960) computed eventual distributions for several countries. Other authors, including Bartholomew (1967) have used the eventual distribution to compute indices of mobility.

Attempts have been made to weaken the assumptions singly or in combinations. Since it has not thus far been possible to test each assumption separately, it may happen that some assumptions will prove justifiable in the absence of others, when more complete data are available. For instance, Hodge (1966) has shown that the Markovian property (4) does not hold for certain inter- and intra-generational data. McFarland (1970) has pointed out that if the data could be reorganized to overcome a possible lumpability effect (see Kemeny and Snell, 1960, Chapter 6), the process might still come out Markovian, but he goes on to argue that the above type of model must be rejected on other grounds.

Matras (1961) incorporated differential fertility in a paper discussed in Section 4.2, and he has more recently (1967) proposed a way to overcome assumptions (1), (5), and (6) by using the growth matrix of the discrete-age demographic model (see Keyfitz, 1968, Chapter 4) to incorporate occupational category with age. I shall make the further bifurcation of the population into persons who have not yet assumed a first job and those who have (although the latter may at some time experience unemployment), which is essential to the evaluation of such a model, and building on Goodman (1968b), give the form of the variance-covariance matrix of the age-occupational distribution, the eventual distribution, and the reproductive values of any category for any other category. This material is presented in Chapter 2.

Another major improvement is a weakening of the homogeneity assumption, described in the "mover-stayer" model of Blumen, Kogan, and McCarthy (1955). We can suppose that there are *two* kinds of persons for each origin: movers, who may change their category over time (but are not required to), and stayers, who are committed to that given category and will never move. If there are J categories, then the diagonal matrix S has, as diagonal entries, the proportion of stayers in each category; $I - S$ will have as diagonal entries the proportion of movers in each category. If M is the stochastic matrix of transition probabilities for the movers, then the transition matrix P for the whole population will be given by $P = S + (I - S)M$. P will be known, but S and M will not be. However, reasonable estimates of these quantities can be obtained (Goodman, 1961). Projection over s intervals of time will then be estimated by the transition matrix $S + (I - S)M^s$. Blumen, Kogan, and McCarthy were able to improve their predictions remarkably through this change.

The mover-stayer model for one mobility pattern uses much different means of estimation of parameters, but is basically equivalent, with the difference that immobility for origin i does not require remaining in category i; it means staying within a region of i, as described earlier. The more restricted definition of immobility by Blumen, Kogan, and McCarthy does not require an ordering of categories. If the categories could be ordered, and if they could be constructed such that the boundaries were nearly equally permeable, then one could generalize to one kind of stayer and $J - 1$ kinds of movers. The diagonal matrix S_0 would give the proportions of stayers in each category and the diagonal matrix S_i would give the proportions of persons in each category who *may* move, but by at most i categories; $\Sigma_i S_i = 1$. If M_i were the transition matrix for i-movers then $P = S_0 + \Sigma_i S_i M_i$. Projection over s intervals of time would be estimated by the transition matrix $S_0 + \Sigma_i S_i M_i^s$. Estimation of parameters would be possible if data were available for a sufficient number of time points. The matrix M_i would have zero entries in all cells more than i rows or columns off the main diagonal.

Blumen, Kogan, and McCarthy suggested a different kind of generalization, which is described more completely by Bartholomew (1967). For a given interval of time (say one year) the population may be heterogeneous according to the number of "decision points" at which the possibility of movement arises. Persons will be stayers except at these points, when they may or may not move. There are good reasons for supposing that the distribution of persons over numbers of decision points in a fixed time interval would be a Poisson distribution. Application of this suggested refinement has been made in a paper by Spilerman (1972).

It would also be possible to subdivide the act of changing category into stages, similar to stages in the adoption of an innovation, a change of attitude, etc. Only actual behavior would be recorded, of course, but the introduction of intermediate stages is attractive for sociological reasons and, mathematically, will yield better predictions (although more parameters are required, so improvement must be balanced against a loss in degrees of freedom). Mayer (1968), Conner (1969), and Goodman (1968b) have made some first steps in this direction.

Another distinct line of alteration of the basic model is elimination of the stationarity assumption. The most distinctive characteristic of a sequence of patterns for an age cohort is the decrease in movement with increased age. The most significant contribution to the incorporation into a model of this well-known trend is due to Mayer (1968). The modification is best made in conjunction with a continuous-time Markov chain (see Karlin, 1968, Chapters 7, 8). The discrete-time chain imposes upon movement an artificially static implication; movement can of course occur at any time during an interval and any time and/or (concomitant) aging effect is continuous (just as under a constant Malthusian rate populations will grow by a continuous exponential, rather than by a discrete geometric function). (Of course, demographic and mobility data are only collected at discrete points in time, so that we can argue for discrete-time models on the grounds of ease of analysis.) Let $P(t)$ be a stochastic transition matrix with continuous entries defined for positive t, which describes how the distribution at time t can be obtained from that at time 0. Associated with such a matrix is an instantaneous generating matrix A(s) (whose rows sum to zero) which is related to P(t) by P(t) = exp $\int_0^t$ A(s)ds or P(t) = I + $\Sigma_{k=0}^\infty$ [$\int_0^t$ A(s)ds] ^{k}/k!. Define B(t) by B(t) = $\int_0^t$ A(s)ds, so that P(t) = I + $\Sigma_{k=0}^\infty$ [B(t)] ^{k}/k!. Iterative methods exist (Mayer, 1968) for estimating B(t_0) given P(t_0), a specific transition matrix from time 0 to time t_0. In some cases one can then estimate P(t) for times other than t = t_0. For example, if the process is stationary, then by definiton A(s) = A, a constant matrix, and B(t) = At. Then A will be estimated by B(t_0)/t_0. Mayer considered the case in which A(s) = Ae^{-at} , in which all entries of the generator are modified by the same negative exponential function of time. Given P(t) for two time points, say t_0 and t_1, it is possible to estimate both A and a and thereby to estimate P(t) for other points in time. Mayer obtained marked improvement over the usual stationary model, despite having to use a synthetic cohort (from a cross-sectional study) for data. Further work with generators which depend upon time, in more complex ways, should be most fruitful.

McGinnis (1968) has suggested use of an enlarged transition matrix which records the number of intervals in which a person has resided in a category. This "Cornell Retention Model" or the "retention model of social mobility" includes the hypothesis that tendency to move declines with increased tenure. Simulation and geographical migration investigations, reported by McGinnis, support this hypothesis. Levine (1969) has used the Blumen, Kogan, and McCarthy occupational mobility data to show that a measure of immobility between pairs of categories decays inversely according to a power of the elapsed time over a two-year period (for each of three five-year age groups). Morrison (1967), using data on residential movement, found evidence that tenure and age interact in predicting movement. Fairly neat analytical forms may be obtained by thus considering higher-order Markov chains for several age groups. Investigations of this sort clearly face challenges in technique and availability of data.

Correspondence with data could be further approached by weakening both the stationarity and homogeneity assumptions at the same time. For example, the parameter of the Poisson distribution over decision frequencies, discussed above, could be made a decreasing function of time (the age of the cohort). It should be clear that any intra-generational model which does not stratify by age, at least, permits a great amount of confounding of the non-homogeneity and non-stationarity implicit in actual mobility.

1.4 Conclusion

Although the models and methods described in this chapter are fairly complicated, they are strictly demographic in nature. Without exception, they could have been rephrased for regional or residential mobility or for movement through any set of categories. In other words, there is no distinctive use of non-ascriptive variables, such as educational aspiration, self-esteem, etc. The over-riding view has been of occupational categories as entities which persist over time, the movement through and between them governed by each individual's history within the set of categories and selected demographic characteristics. It is satisfying that with such a skeletal view of social mobility we are able to detect patterns and regularities.

There are many questions about social mobility, however, to which this structural, demographic approach can never yield answers. Many answers probably lie in an extension of the Blau and Duncan (1967) use of a continuous prestige scale. In particular, we could take as the components of an analysis (a) a bivariate or trivariate continuous vector, in which the aspects of status are kept separate, to allow for the possibility of status inconsistency; (b) evaluation of this vector over a long period of time for each individual, tracing out his career, beginning with first job; (c) parallel to this time series, another vector function of time recording theoretically relevant variables which change over time; and (d) for each individual a vector of background characteristics, such as parental statuses and education, standing prior to the two time series. The choice of variables and postulated links could be evaluated with methods of econometrics, going beyond the linear model. Some of the methods encountered in this book could be extended to incorporate these additional characteristics of individuals (using methods described by Haberman, 1974).

There is a desirable complementarity between use of the nominal-ordinal variable of occupational category and use of a continuous (perhaps multivariate) variable of prestige or status. The former is far better able to integrate movement with changes in demographic supply and in technological demand, by the use of persistent categories. On the other hand, the latter, by re-standardizing the individual's statuses at each time inverval against the distribution of these statuses over the whole population, can describe how it may happen that a person who has held the same occupation through his whole career may actually have declined in prestige and been downwardly mobile, for example.

In this chapter I have sought to define the research context of the work described later herein. This research tradition is admittedly a peculiar one within sociology. This peculiarity may be stated in terms of the nearly exclusive use of ascriptive variables, as above. The aggregate structure of mobility is considered in isolation from its sociological determinants and consequences. Questions such as the following, for example, are foreign to this tradition: How do the political ideology and system affect, and how are they affected by, the pattern of mobility? How does a "culture of poverty" relate to patterns of mobility? What kinds of cultural change are modified by mobility patterns, and in what way? What is the role of mobility in the assimilation of minorities? How strongly are life styles associated with occupational membership, and how do these styles, or constellations of attitudes and behaviors, tend to change as a person changes occupation or status? Issues such as the above, some of which are inter-related, and many others, are imbedded in other research traditions.

Yet the issues raised in this chapter and represented by the studies cited above are, I believe, logically, if not historically, prior to all substantive questions that revolve about aggregates of movement. This can be illustrated with a simple analogy. Suppose that one wished to relate the aggregate fertility of a dozen U.S. ethnic or racial groups to their respective educational levels. Putting aside a possible ecological fallacy, at the very least one would control for the age-sex composition of the groups by some technique such as standardization, to avoid the simple effects of recent immigration, previous high periods of fertility which would have affected the present age distribution, etc.

The present work, part of a general effort to identify and control for structural variables, is viewed as an antecedent to future work which will integrate aggregate patterns of movement into an inter-related system of more properly sociological variables. The tradition represented herein is of value insofar as it eventually moves toward that end.

CHAPTER 2

The discrete-time model for mobility

2.1 Introduction

The model presented herein is basically an elaboration of the familiar demographic model of Lotka (see Keyfitz, 1968, Chapters 2, 3) for population growth, which has age-specific mortality and fertility rates (for one sex only) as its inputs. The growth process over, say, a ten-year interval can be described equivalently with a matrix and vector format as a branching process (see Harris, 1963, Chapter 1) or, as Goodman has shown (1967), with a set of recurrent equations. The latter description has an unexpected elegance for growth models because so many kinds of transitions have zero probability (e.g., in theory, at least, one cannot age 20 years in 10 elapsed years of time). The matrix and vector format will be used here, for most (although not all) purposes.

The elaboration is quite straightforward, and proceeds in two steps. The first step is the introduction of a dichotomous classification, post-entry vs. pre-entry, which simply describes whether or not a person has yet held a first full-time job. The second step is the introduction of various occupational groups, including a category of unemployed and retired workers.

2.2 The incorporation of first job

Divide the population into two categories: Type 0, pre-entry, and Type 1, post-entry. The population is also divided into age groups, denoted by $\bar{0}, \bar{1}, \bar{2}$, etc. Persons of Type 1 are in age groups $\bar{1}, \ldots, \bar{I}$; i.e., for Type 1, age group $\bar{0}$ is empty and age group $\bar{I}$ is the oldest non-empty age group. Persons of Type 0 are only in age groups $\bar{0}, \bar{1}, \ldots, \bar{K}$; i.e., for Type 0, age group $\bar{K}$ is the oldest non-empty age group. Assume $K \leqslant I$.

Notation for the distribution vector at time t (this is not a *probability* distribution vector) is developed as follows. Let $n_{\delta t}(x)$ be the number of persons at age x at time t who are pre-entry $(\delta = 0)$ or post-entry $(\delta = 1)$, and define the $I + K + 1 \times 1$ column vector

$$n_t = \begin{pmatrix} n_{0t}(0) \\ \vdots \\ n_{0t}(K) \\ n_{1t}(1) \\ \vdots \\ n_{1t}(I) \end{pmatrix}$$

Then n_t gives the distribution of persons over age and entry status categories.

Possible kinds of movement and their respective probabilities are given as follows:

For a post-entry person in the x-th age interval $(x = 1, \ldots, I)$ at time t,

(a) The probability is $\phi_{i1}(x)$ that he will survive to the $(x + 1)$-th age interval at time $t + 1$ and will also produce i persons who will be pre-entry and of age 0 at time $t + 1$. $(\phi_{i1}(I) = 0$ for all i.)

(b) The probability is $\phi_{i2}(x)$ that he will die during the time period t to $t + 1$ but will produce i persons who will be pre-entry and of age 0 at time $t + 1$.

For a pre-entry person in the x-th age interval $(x = 0, \ldots, K)$ at time t,

(c) The probability is $a(x)$ that he will survive to the $(x + 1)$-th age interval at time $t + 1$ and will remain pre-entry. $(a(K) = 0.)$

(d) The probability is $h(x)$ that he will survive to the $(x + 1)$-th age interval at time $t + 1$ but will become post-entry.

We make some additional definitions:

$$m(x) = \Sigma_i \phi_{i1}(x) \qquad\qquad x = 1, \ldots, I-1$$

$$b(x) = \Sigma_i i[\phi_{i1}(x) + \phi_{i2}(x)] = \Sigma_i i\phi_{i\cdot}(x) \qquad x = 1, \ldots, I$$

$$u_1(x) = \Sigma_i \phi_{i2}(x) \qquad\qquad x = 1, \dots, I$$

$$u_2(x) = 1 - a(x) - h(x) \qquad\qquad x = 0, \dots, K$$

All of these quantities are expected values:
$m(x)$ is the fraction of post-entry persons aged x who will survive to age $x + 1$; $b(x)$ is the number of births to each post-entry person aged x; $u_1(x)$ is the fraction of post-entry persons aged x who will not survive to age $x + 1$; $u_2(x)$ is the fraction of pre-entry persons aged x who will not survive to age $x + 1$.

Let A_{IK} be the matrix of expected values, i.e., the matrix of the transformation which takes n_t into n_{t+1}. This matrix is found at once to be

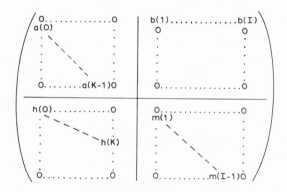

The lower right-hand block is $I \times I$; the lower left-hand block is $I \times (K + 1)$; the upper left-hand block is $(K + 1) \times (K + 1)$; the upper right-hand block is $(K + 1) \times I$.

Thus $n_{t+1} = A_{IK} n_t$. If we were to proceed as in the theory of stable population growth we would assume that (1) the probabilities above are independent of t, (2) the sub-populations generated by two co-existing individuals develop independently of one another, (3) the process is first-order Markovian. Then we would have a Galton-Watson branching process. The asymptotic and stochastic implications of these assumptions are presented in Appendix 2.

2.3 The introduction of occupational categories

Because most data are dichotomized on employment status rather than on "post-first job vs. pre-first job", the previous growth model has primary use as a prelude to the following more elaborate model. Note that movement from Type 1 to Type 0 is by births only. Note also that persons of Type 0 are assumed not to give birth. This may be viewed as a defect in the model, but actually it simplifies computation considerably. Empirically it is established that employment nearly always precedes childbearing. Particularly since application will normally be to five- or ten-year age intervals, error incurred by ignoring children born to pre-employed persons should be negligible. Also, because the number of persons who never take a first job is so small, the assumption $K \leqslant I$ can be interpreted to mean that if a first job has not been taken by age 35, say, then a person is placed in the post-employed category but as an unemployed person.

J occupational groups (one of which is the category of un-employed) are introduced and transition rates are defined as follows:

For a post-entry person in the x-th age interval ($x = 1, \ldots, I$) and occ. j at time t,

(a) The probability is $\phi_{ij'j1}(x)$ that he will survive to the $(x + 1)$-th age interval and occ. j' and will also produce i persons who will be pre-entry and of age 0, occ. j' at time $t + 1$. ($\phi_{ij'j1}(1) = 0$ for all i, j, and j'.)

(b) The probability is $\phi_{ij2}(x)$ that he will die during the time interval t to $t + 1$ but will produce i persons who will be pre-entry and of age 0, occ. j at time t.

For a pre-entry person in the x-th age interval ($x = 0, \ldots, K$) and occ. j at time t,

(c) The probability is $a_j(x)$ that he will survive to the $(x + 1)$-th age interval and occ. j at time $t + 1$, remaining pre-entry. ($a_j(K) = 0$ for all j.)

(d) The probability is $h_{j'j}(x)$ that he will survive to the $(x + 1)$-th age interval and occ. j' at time $t + 1$, becoming post-entry.

(a) and (b) involve intra-generational mobility; (d) involves inter-generational mobility.

We define the following quantities:

$$b_{j'j}(x) = \Sigma_i i \phi_{ij'j1}(x) \qquad\qquad \text{if } j \neq j'$$

$$b_{jj}(x) = \Sigma_i i [\phi_{ijj1}(x) + \phi_{ij2}(x)]$$

$$m_{j'j}(x) = \Sigma_i \phi_{ij'j1}(x)$$

26

$$H(x) = |\, b_{j'j}(x)\,|_{J \times J}$$

$$B(x) = |b_{j'j}(x)|_{J \times J} \qquad A(x) = \begin{pmatrix} a(1) \cdots 0 \\ \ddots \\ 0 \cdots a(I) \end{pmatrix} \quad n_t = \begin{pmatrix} n_{0t}(0) \\ \vdots \\ n_{0t}(K) \\ n_{1t}(1) \\ \vdots \\ n_{1t}(I) \end{pmatrix}$$

$$M(x) = |m_{j'j}(x)|_{J \times J}$$

where each component of n_t is a $J \times 1$ vector and

$$n_{\delta t}(k) = \begin{pmatrix} n_{\delta 1 t}(k) \\ \vdots \\ n_{\delta J t}(k) \end{pmatrix}$$

for $\delta = 0$ or 1.

In the above, $b_{j'j}(x)$ is the expected number of pre-entry persons with occupation j' and age 0 at time $t + 1$ who are born per post-entry person with occupation j and age x at time t; $m_{j'j}(x)$ is the expected proportion of post-entry persons with occupation j and age x at time t who are post-entry with occupation j' and age $x + 1$ at time $t + 1$.

Under these definitions the structure of the matrix of expected values will be identical with that of the previous model with the elements of the latter replaced by $J \times J$ sub-matrices. That is,

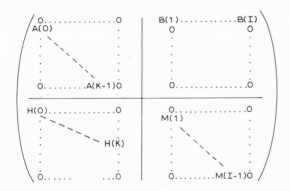

Here 0 represents a $J \times J$ matrix, all of whose elements are zero. Thus $n_{t+1} = A_{IKJ} n_t$. If we make the assumptions leading to the description of this process as a Galton-Watson branching process, including the assumption of quasi-positive regularity (see Good-

27

man, 1968a, p. 475), we can compute various stochastic and asymptotic results. These are presented in Appendix 2.

This model is similar to a model by Matras (1967). However, Matras does not introduce the concept of first occupation. He thereby (1) permits children to move independently of their fathers *prior* to actual entry into the labor force and (2) complicates the application of the model to data for those age groups when the first job is usually taken on. Our model shares with that of Matras the incorporation of inter-generational and intra-generational change of class into a single format and the replacement of the imprecise concept of the generation by fixed time intervals, e.g., five or ten years. It shares with all matrix models, since their introduction by Prais (1955), the unordered view of occupational categories. This approach also emphasizes that the proper element of inter-generational mobility studies is *lines of descent,* or family trees.

According to the formal definitions, children are identified with the occupation of the father while the child was in age group $\overline{0}$ (e.g., ages 0−10) if the father was alive then, or with the occupation of the father at the time the child was born, if the father did not survive the birth of the child. That is, the B matrices need not be diagonal in form. A diagonal form for the B matrices, with zeroes in all off-diagonal cells, would not allow for occupational movement of fathers during the interval when sons were born.

If it were desired to identify the child with the occupation of the father while the child was in age group 1 (e.g., ages 10−20), slight alterations would be required. We can assume that class-specific birth rates do not depend on whether a person stays or moves or dies during a given interval, nor on where he moves. This assumption will induce some error, since fertility patterns, like most behavior, tend to be intermediate to the origin and destination categories, (see Hope, 1971). However, we can take it as a good first approximation.

Let $B^0(x) = |b^0{}_{j'j}(x)|$ be the J x J matrix of class-specific expectations of boys born during an interval to men of age x and category j, with elements defined by

$$b^0{}_{j'j}(x) = \begin{cases} b_j(x) \text{ if } j = j' \\ 0 \text{ if } j \neq j' \end{cases}$$

Then it is easily verified that $B(x) = M(x)B^0(x)$, where B and M are defined as above. To keep sons with fathers for the extra interval of time (at least in terms of expected movement), three changes must be made. First, each $B(x)$ in the A_{IKJ} matrix should be replaced by the 0 matrix. Second, the second row of the upper right quadrant of the A_{IKJ} matrix should have its 0 (matrix) elements successively replaced by the matrices

$$B(x) = M(x)A(x-1)M(x-1)B^0(x-1) \text{ for } x = 1, \dots, I.$$

This alteration accounts for the birth of children one age interval (of the father) earlier, the movement of the father across two time periods, and the survival of the child to the second time interval, according to the assumption of independence above; survival rates used are specific to the category of the father when the child was in age group $\bar{0}$. Third, a change should be made in the transition process. By carrying sons along we change the process to a second, rather than first order Markov chain. An easy algorithm for carrying out this change is as follows: whenever $B(x)$ is to be multiplied (on the right) by a component vector of the n_t vector, multiply it instead by the corresponding component vector of the n_{t-1} vector. Of course, if there is little difference between the n_t and n_{t-1} vectors, then the effect of this third change will be small; typically, the two successive vectors will have very similar distributions, and will differ primarily by a multiplicative factor (the main growth effect).

CHAPTER 3

Forced mobility

3.1 Objective

In Chapter 1 a distinction was made between two ways of viewing mobility. We shall briefly review the distinction in order to bring out parallels in development of the two perspectives. The first perspective takes the continuous variable of present socio-economic status as a dependent variable and attempts to reduce the (conditional) variance of this variable by conditioning on several independent variables, i.e., variables which are presumed relevant and which are temporally or theoretically prior. Linear regression analysis is one (though not the only) technique for conditioning on a set of prior variables, thus, in a sense, "removing their effect" on the dependent variable. Linear regression is a plausible model, nothing more. Even if all other effects could be removed, it is doubtful that the relationship between two variables (e.g., present SES and father's education) would be best represented by a straight line.

Thus, under the first perspective, the procedure employed is essentially to divide a given individual's present SES into two components: one is the "predicted" SES, i.e., the SES implied by a linear, "reasonable" model for evaluating the implications of the prior variables, and the "error", which reflects the attainment due to unmeasured variables, and randomness.

The second perspective employs an ordinal or nominal occupational variable and employs methods for the analysis of cross-classified data. It is our objective here to extend the second perspective in the same sense as the first, although much different methods must be used. That is, we wish to divide mobility rates into two parts, the first reflecting the implications of variables defined to be prior, and the second reflecting movement due to unmeasured variables, and randomness.

Kahl (1957) delineated four sources of mobility: three structural sources — differential fertility rates, changes in the occupational distribution, immigration — and a residual source, "circulation". Of course, it is impossible to say whether a given individual has been mobile for structural reasons or through circulation. But a measure of the mobility implied by structural factors is an indicator of the openness of the system since if all mobility were implied by changes in the occupational distribution, presumably required by technological changes, or by class-specific fertility differences, then surely comments on the openness of the system would require revision.

Another use of the separation of effects is in its indication of the permanence of the mobility pattern. In the 1940's Sibley (1942) speculated on the impact upon future mobility of reduced immigration into the United States. Immigration had induced considerable mobility and it was believed that without this source of new persons in the less skilled categories, who had to be shuffled into higher levels, there would be considerably less gross mobility. As it happened, this structural factor was replaced in importance by the post-war growth of white-collar categories.

These writers appear to have overlooked mobility which is due to interaction between career patterns as individuals grow older and population changes in the age distribution. Any patterns that may help us to describe movement from first occupation on through last occupation will clearly be affected if the age structure becomes markedly older or markedly younger in the space of a generation. The phenomenon referred to here is similar to the one which has led many contemporary adults of late-middle age to feel passed over because during their youth, values were set by adults but now, they feel, values are set by young people. To give an illustration in our own context: suppose that upward mobility dominates as a person grows older in the United States (as, in fact, it does, for largely structural reasons). If we hold the occupational distribution constant for a time but increase the number of younger persons and reduce the number of older persons, it will be necessary for some young persons to take on "higher" categories early in their careers and the upwardly mobile gross *intra*-generational mobility rates will be reduced (see Keyfitz, 1973).

If fertility rates are introduced over time as well as over class and if mortality rates are introduced, we can incorporate changes in the age distribution as a structural input. The procedure employed herein, however, for short-run analysis, will be to take an initial age distribution at t_0 and to compute the distribution at a later time from the fertility-mortality schedule at t_0. We can then inquire about the implied effects of the changed distribution. Since the age distribution will change markedly during the rest of this century as a consequence (largely) of the post-war baby boom, the potency of this change as a source of intra-generational mobility, in particular, is worth investigation.

3.2 The elementary case: the Matras analysis

The crude inter-generational mobility table has the following form:

Sons are sampled, and n_{ij} is the number of sons with occupation j whose fathers held occupation i at some point in time, for example when the son was born or was fifteen years old. We define $n_{i.} = \Sigma_j n_{ij}$ and $n_{.j} = \Sigma_i n_{ij}$ and $N = \Sigma_i \Sigma_j n_{ij}$. The proportion immobile is $P_I = \Sigma_i n_{ii}/N$ and the proportion mobile is $P_m = 1 - P_I$. If the J categories were ordered by status then we clearly could subdivide P_m into proportion upwardly and proportion downwardly mobile. Because of variations in age of respondent and in age of father at time of respondent's birth, as well as because of differential fertility (for example, men who have no sons at all cannot possibly be represented in the conventional table), the marginal distribution of fathers does not reflect directly the population distribution at any point in time. These complexities have been discussed further by Duncan (1966). We will temporarily overlook these confounding effects and will refer to the sampling date as t_1, assuming that "Father's Category" does refer to a specific point in time, t_0. We assume a system closed to immigration and emigration.

32

Note that the information in the crude table could be conveyed by a matrix equation, since $n_{.j} = \Sigma_i n_{ij} = \Sigma_i (n_{ij}/n_{i.}) n_{i.}$.
Thus if we define

$$p_{ij} = n_{ij}/n_{i.} ,$$

$$n_i^t = \begin{cases} n_{i.} \text{ if } t = 0 \\ n_{.j} \text{ if } t = 1 \end{cases}$$

$$n^t = \begin{pmatrix} n_1^t \\ \vdots \\ n_J^t \end{pmatrix} , \quad t = 0, 1,$$

$$P = |p_{ij}|$$

then $n^1 = P'n^0$. (It is more common in mathematical statistics to represent the marginal distributions by row vectors so that P, a stochastic matrix, describes the transformation. Because the mathematical theory is here integrated with the theory of population growth in which column vectors are more conventional, we use column vectors.)

The following is due primarily to Kahl (1957) and Matras (1961). Suppose that in addition to the above two vectors we are given m^0, the vector whose i-th entry is the number of persons in the total population at t_0 who were in occ. category i. Overlooking confounding effects temporarily, m^0 gives the distribution of fathers at t_1, in contrast to n^0, which gives the distribution of sons by father's occupation at t_0. If m is the sum of the components m_i^0 of m, then $(1/m)\, m^0$ is a probability distribution vector. Further, suppose that we are given the net reproduction rate, R_i, for each category i during the fathers' reproductive period. That is, $R = (1/m) \cdot \Sigma_i m_i^0 R_i$ is the net reproduction rate for the entire population. At once we have the following relationship: $n_i^0 = R_i m_i^0$, so that $R = n/m$. Consequently any two of the three sets of n_i^0's, m_i^0's and R_i's will yield the third. We can introduce (as Matras does) a fourth set of numbers, $G_1, \ldots, G_J$, through the relations $n_i^1 = G_i m_i^0$. Thus, G_i is the proportion of growth in category i, from t_0 (fathers) to t_1 (sons).

Given the three distribution vectors, three pairwise comparisons exist and are of possible interest. We shall make these comparisons through indices of dissimilarity, computed after standardization of the vectors into *probability* distribution vectors (see Duncan and Duncan, 1955).

33

Due to the differential fertility alone, the vectors m^0 and n^0 differ, despite their common reference in time. The proportional shift between the standardized vectors, i.e., the fraction of sons (as children) who would be forced to move in order to replicate their fathers' distribution, is

$$\Delta(n^0, m^0) = \tfrac{1}{2}\Sigma \, |(n_i^0/n) - (m_i^0/m)|$$

$$= \tfrac{1}{2}\Sigma \, |(R_i m_i^0/Rm) - (m_i^0/m)|$$

$$= \tfrac{1}{2}\Sigma(m_i^0/m) \, |(R_i/R) - 1|$$

$$\text{or } \tfrac{1}{2}\Sigma(n_i^0/n) \, |1 - (R/R_i)| \, .$$

Due to differential growth of categories alone, the vectors m^0 and n^1 differ. The proportional shift between the standardized vectors, i.e., the fraction of sons (as adults) who would be forced to move in order to replicate their father's distribution, is

$$\Delta(m^0, n^1) = \tfrac{1}{2}\Sigma|(m_i^0/m) - (n_i/n)|$$

$$= \tfrac{1}{2}\Sigma|(m_i^0/m) - (G_i m_i^0/Rm)|$$

$$= \tfrac{1}{2}\Sigma(m_i^0/m)|1 - (G_i/R)|$$

$$\text{or } \tfrac{1}{2}\Sigma(n_i^0/n)|(R/R_i) - (G_i/R_i)| \, .$$

It is worthwhile to compare $\Delta(n^0, n^1)$ with P_m. Matras (1961) found that although P_m varies widely from country to country, $P_m - \Delta(n^0, n^1)$, the unforced or circulatory level or mobility, is relatively constant, indicating a similarity in circulatory mobility patterns.

We can introduce here a concept not discussed by Matras, which does not explicitly require an inter-generational mobility table and which does not involve the complications deriving from the sampling of sons alone, since the R_i's and G_i's are based on census, rather than sample data. It can happen that for class i, $R_i > R$, so that in a relative sense a "surplus" of individuals are born into class i, and that, in addition, $G_i < R$, i.e., there is a reduced "demand" for persons of class i. In this event differential fertility and distributional change will be said to *reinforce* each other because either inequality, in the presence of the other, forces per-

34

sons *out of* class i. Similarly, if $R_i < R$ and $G_i > R$ then the effects reinforce each other, because either inequality in the presence of the other forces persons *into* class i. The only other configurations, $R_i > R$ and $G_i > R$, or $R_i < R$ and $G_i < R$, will be considered indicative of a *compensating* relation between the effects.

Now if $R_i > R$ and $R > G_i$, then it is easy to verify that $|(R_i/R) - 1| + |1 - (G_i/R)| = |(R_i/R) - (G_i/R)|$. This result will also hold for the other instance of reinforcement, i.e., $R > R_i$ and $G_i > R$. A different result holds if the two effects are compensating. We can subdivide into two subcases. First, if $R_i > G_i > R$ or $R > G_i > R_i$, then $|(R_i/R) - 1| - |1 - (G_i/R)| = |(R_i/R) - (G_i/R)|$. Second, if $G_i > R_i > R$ or $R > R_i > G_i$, then $|(R_i/R) - 1| - |1 - (G_i/R)| = |(R_i/R) - (G_i/R)|$. In the former compensating case, differential fertility has dominated. In the latter case, differential growth of categories has dominated.

In view of these relations it is possible to clarify how the single-effect measures, $\Delta(n^0, m^0)$, and $\Delta(m^0, n^1)$, are related to the combined effect measure, $\Delta(n^0, n^1)$. If, for category i, the effects are reinforcing, then $\Delta_i(n^0, m^0) + \Delta_i(m^0, n^1) = \Delta_i(n^0, n^1)$, where Δ_i indicates the part of Δ due to category i. If, for category i, the effects are compensating, but $R_i > G_i$, then $\Delta_i(n^0, m^0) - \Delta_i(m^0, n^1) = \Delta_i(n^0, n^1)$. If, for category i, the effects are compensating, but $R_i < G_i$, then $\Delta_i(n^0, m^0) - \Delta_i(m^0, n^1) = -\Delta_i(n^0, n^1)$. In this way we are able to evaluate in an aggregate way the relative importance of differential fertility and differential growth and the relative importance of reinforcement and compensation between these effects. To do this we proceed through the following steps:

(1) Divide the set I of occupational groups into three subsets:
   I_a, in which the effects are reinforcing,
   I_b, in which the effects are compensating and differential fertility has dominated,
   I_c, in which the effects are compensating and differential growth of categories has dominated.

(2) Consider

$$\tfrac{1}{2}\Sigma(m_i^0/m_i) |(R_i/R) - (G_i/R)| \quad \text{or} \quad \tfrac{1}{2}\Sigma(n_i^0/n_i) |1 - (G_i/R_i)|.$$

Let Δ_a, Δ_b, and Δ_c be the value of this quantity when the summation is restricted to I_a, I_b, and I_c, respectively. Then $\Delta(n^0, n^1) = \Delta_a + \Delta_b + \Delta_c$. The ratios γ_a, γ_b, and γ_c, defined by $\gamma_. = (\Delta_./\Delta(n^0, n^1))$ so that $1 = \gamma_a + \gamma_b + \gamma_c$, indicate the relative importance of reinforcement of effects and the two types of compensation. (Here a dot (·) subscript does not indicate summing or averaging but simply holds a place for a, b, or c.)

(3) On the other hand,

$$\Delta(n^0, n^1) = \tfrac{1}{2}\Sigma_I (m_i^0/m) \, |(R_i/R) - (G_i/R)|$$

$$= \tfrac{1}{2}[\Sigma_{I_a} + \Sigma_{I_b} + \Sigma_{I_c}] \, (m_i^0/m) \, |(R_i/R) - (G_i/R)|$$

$$= \tfrac{1}{2}[\Sigma_{I_a} + \Sigma_{I_b} - \Sigma_{I_c}] \, (m_i^0/m) \, |(R_i/R) - 1|$$

$$+ \tfrac{1}{2}[\Sigma_{I_a} - \Sigma_{I_b} + \Sigma_{I_c}] \, (m_i^0/m) \, |1 - (G_i/R)|.$$

Let $\Delta_R = \tfrac{1}{2}[\Sigma_{I_a} + \Sigma_{I_b} - \Sigma_{I_c}] \, (m_i^0/m) \, |1 - (G_i/R)|$ and let $\Delta_G = \Delta(n^0, n^1) - \Delta_R$. Then $(n^0, n^1) = \Delta_R + \Delta_G$ and the ratios δ_R and δ_G, defined by $\delta_. = \Delta_./\Delta(n^0, n^1)$, so that $1 = \delta_R + \delta_G$, indicate the relative importance of differential fertility and differential growth.

Table 8, for which Kahl reports $R = 1.27$, demonstrates that between 1920 and 1950 approximately two-thirds of the United

TABLE 8.

Occupational distribution of first generation adults ($\tfrac{1}{m} m_i^0$); net reproduction rates by occupational group (R_i); and generation growth rates for occupational groups (G_i).*

Occupation Groups	i	$\tfrac{1}{m} m_i^0$	R_i	G_i
Professional Persons	1	0.032	0.87	1.75
Proprietors, Managers and Officials				
Farmers	2	0.187	1.52	0.42
Others	3	0.080	0.98	1.02
Clerks, Sales People, and Kindred	4	0.106	0.98	0.94
Skilled Workers and Foremen	5	0.167	1.22	0.87
Semi-Skilled Workers	6	0.133	1.18	1.28
Unskilled Workers				
Farm Laborers	7	0.096	1.52	0.39
Others	8	0.198	1.35	0.52

*Adapted from J. A. Kahl, *The American Class Structure*, Chapter IX, Table 2.

$\Delta(n^0, n^1) = 0.230$ $\gamma_a = 0.889$

$\delta_R = 0.164$ $\gamma_b = 0.005$

$\delta_G = 0.836$ $\gamma_c = 0.106$

36

States labor force were in occupational groups in which the effects reinforced one another. Moreover, these categories were associated with extremes of status. The quantities Δ_a, Δ_b, Δ_c, Δ_R, and Δ_G are given for this table. They tell us that of the sons of the men in the table, 23 per cent were *required* to shift position (we are not told how many actually did shift). Differential growth of categories was roughly five times as important as differential fertility in impact on moves. When the two factors compensated one another the first factor was dominant even more often; but about 90 per cent of the forced movement was due to reinforcement of the two factors.

These quantities may be better understood if compared with corresponding values under appropriate null models. (1) If there were no differential fertility over classes, i.e., if $R_i = R$ for all i, then a proportion $(0.836) (0.230) = 0.192$ would be required to move. If there were no differential growth, i.e., if $G_i = R$ for all i, then only a proportion $(0.164) (0.230) = 0.038$ would be required to move. (2) If there were differential fertility and growth but they were not inversely correlated over classes, as they empirically are, and if they were each symmetrically distributed *over the population* about their means R, which is a reasonable standard for comparison, then it is easily shown that γ_a, γ_b, and γ_c would take the values 0.50, 0.25, and 0.25 respectively.

3.3 The discrete-time extension

Section 3.2 was based entirely on the comparison of three vectors, n^0, n^1, and m^0, as defined on page 33. Times 0 and 1 referred to the early date of socialization of a cohort and to that cohort's date of maturation, respectively; i.e., 0 and 1 were the end-points of a generation, loosely defined. The vectors n^0 and n^1 referred to the same cohort at two points in time and m^0 referred to the cohort's fathers at time 0. By applying data on the labor force in 1920 and 1950 to the model we made the assumption that the 1920 data referred to a cohort of fathers and the 1950 data to a cohort of sons.

In this section we partially overcome this defect by introducing (1) age, and (2) post- or pre-entry into the labor force. We also reduce the interval of time from thirty years (or a generation) to five or ten years. (On the basis of the U.S. data reported in Chapter 6, ten-year intervals are considered preferable to five-year intervals, even though most age-specific data are based on five-year intervals.

This conclusion is based on the low amounts of mobility, even under narrow definitions of categories, that occur over a five-year interval.) It is our objective (1) to determine how much mobility was "forced", (2) to classify the forced cases into various subtypes, and (3) to compare the forced actual movement for a set of data.

We shall return to the notation of Chapter 2. A generic frequency is $n_{\delta jt}(k)$, where δ takes the value 0 for pre-entry and 1 for post-entry.

j = occupational group $1, \ldots, J$
t = time
k = age group $0, \ldots, K$ if $\delta = 0$; $1, \ldots, I$ if $\delta = 1$; $K < I$.

We can make the following definitions:

$$A_{\delta t}(k) = \Sigma_j n_{\delta jt}(k) \qquad \text{for } \delta = 0, 1$$

$$N_{\delta jt} = \Sigma_k n_{\delta jt}(k) \qquad \text{for } \delta = 0, 1$$

We interpret $A_{0t}(1), \ldots, A_{0t}(I)$ as the age distribution of pre-entry persons; $A_{1t}(0), \ldots, A_{1t}(K)$ as the age distribution of post-entry persons (at time t). Next, $N_{\delta 1t}, \ldots, N_{\delta jt}$ is the occupational distribution of pre-entry ($\delta = 0$) or post-entry ($\delta = 1$) persons (at time t). Then

$$[A_{0, t+1}(k+1) + A_{1, t+1}(k+1)]/[A_{0t}(k) + A_{1t}(k)] = S_{kt}$$

is the mean age-specific survival rate from age k at time t to age k + 1 at time t + 1.

$[N_{1j, t+1}]/[N_{1jt}] = G_{jt}$ is the proportional growth in occupation j from time t to time t + 1.

$$[\Sigma_{\delta, k} A_{\delta, t+1}(k)]/[\Sigma_{\delta, k} A_{\delta t}(k)] = [\Sigma_{\delta, j} N_{\delta j, t+1}]/[\Sigma_{\delta, j} N_{\delta jt}] = R_t$$

is the proportional increase in the total population from time t to time t + 1. Now observe that $A_{1, t+1}(k+1)$, the number of post-entry persons of age k + 1 at time t + 1, will be composed exclusively as follows:

(1) if k + 1 = 1: by persons who are pre-entry, age 0 at time t;

(2) if $k + 1 = 2, \ldots,$ or $K + 1$: by persons who were of age k at time t but either post- or pre-entry;

(3) if $k + 1 = K + 2, \ldots, I$: by persons who were post-entry, age k at time t.

Depending on the value of k, the above determines the "antecedent" categories for age group $A_{1,t+1}(k)$, in that $A_{1,t+1}(k)$ is comprised solely of persons who are in these categories.

If we are willing to assume that the joint distribution of post-entry ages and occupations was constrained by the larger system, then the total proportion of forced movement as n^t was transformed into n^{t+1} was composed of three parts:

(1) if $k + 1 = 1$ (i.e., if $k = 0$):

$$\tfrac{1}{2}\Sigma_j |[n_{0jt}(0)/A_{0t}(0)] - [n_{1j,\,t+1}(1)/A_{1,\,t+1}(1)]| = \Delta_t(0)$$

(2) if $k + 1 = 2, \ldots,$ or $K + 1$ (i.e., if $k = 1,\ldots, K$):

$$\tfrac{1}{2}\Sigma_j |[(n_{0jt}(k) + n_{ijt}(k)]/(A_{0t}(k) + A_{1t}(k))$$

$$- [n_{ij,\,t+1}(k + 1)/A_{1,\,t+1}(k + 1)]| = \Delta_t(k)$$

(3) if $k + 1 = K + 2, \ldots, I$ (i.e., if $k = K + 1, \ldots, I - 1$):

$$\tfrac{1}{2}\Sigma_j |[n_{1jt}(k)/A_{1t}(k)] - [n_{1j,\,t+1}(k + 1)/A_{1,\,t+1}(k+1)]| = \Delta_t(k)$$

Each of these proportions is computed on a base of the number of survivors of the antecedent sub-population. If we wish to obtain a proportion for the entire antecedent population, which will include all persons at time t except those in the post-entry, age I category, then we compute a weighted sum of the above Δ's:

$$\Delta_t = \big\{ A_{0,\,t+1}(0)\Delta_t(0) + \Sigma_{k=1}^{K} [A_{0,\,t+1}(k) + A_{1,\,t+1}(k)]\Delta_t(k)$$

$$+ \Sigma_{k=K+1}^{I-1} A_{1,\,t+1}(k)\Delta_t(k)\big\} [\Sigma_{k=0}^{K} A_{0,\,t+1}(k) + \Sigma_{k=1}^{I-1} A_{1,\,t+1}(k)]$$

If the age-specific mobility matrices are available as assumed in Chapter 2, then it is possible to compute the proportions *actually* mobile from each age and entry-status origin. Let $p_{\delta t}(k)$ be the proportion of the survivors of the antecedent population with age k and entry-status δ who at time $t + 1$ are post-entry and in a *different* occupational category than at time t. Then,

(1) if $k + 1 = 1$: $p_{1t}(0) - \Delta_t(0) = D_t(0)$

(2) if $k + 1 = 2, \ldots, K + 1$:

$[A_{0,t+1}(k)p_{1t}(k) + A_{1,t+1}(k)p_{0t}(k)] / [A_{0,t+1}(k) + A_{1,t+1}(k)]$
$- \Delta_t(k) = D_t(k)$

(3) if $K + 1 = K + 2, \ldots, I$: $p_{0t}(k) - \Delta_t(k) = D_t(k)$

then $D_t(k)$ is the excess of actual over required mobility.

Category (1) above relates to purely inter-generational movement, and category (3) relates to purely intra-generational movement, but category (2), involving K values of k, $k = 1, \ldots, K$, relates to a combination of the two, i.e., involves some cases of movement from father's occupation to first occupation, and some cases of subsequent movement. Depending on the kind of data available, it may or may not be possible to separate the two types in the category. If such a separation is possible, then it is a straight-forward matter to compute the "forced" shift for each sub-population at each age, $k = 1, \ldots, K$. Comparisons between sub-populations, for each age, using "forced" and "residual" shifts, could be made. (Residuals should decrease with age but be consistently lower for intra-generational movement than for inter-generational movement.)

In developing a measure of "forced" movement it is necessary to assume that certain constraints have operated on the destination vector. It may be appealing to assume that the joint age and destination vector is determined down to its last entry, as in Case 1, because of the relative simplicity. This assumption is extremely strong, however. It is plausible to require a fixed age distribution, implied by the mortality and fertility schedules, and to require a fixed occupational distribution. Since persons of a wide range of ages are found in all occupational groups (if not in all occupations) we suggest relaxing the constraints on the joint distribution. If we assume nothing about how age and occupation are jointly articulated at time $t + 1$, however, then virtually nothing can be added beyond the techniques of 3.2, for (1) we cannot define any age-specific measures, and (2) as a consequence of (1) we cannot even separate inter- from intra-generational movement.

At this point a re-examination of the concept of "forced" movement, as described in Chapter 2, is required. Kahl and Matras have structured the phenomenon solely in terms of the marginal distribution for occupations. It is easy to incorporate constraints on the marginal age distribution. But it is a major substantive assumption that the joint distribution is constrained, simply because it is the distribution we observe. Yet the incorporation of age is a major refinement of the discrete-time model, and if we cannot articulate age with occupation in a "forced" destination vector, then an apparent refinement becomes a barrier which casts doubt on the entire conceptualization. It is for this reason that we now change our focus from "forced" movement to the residual or circulatory pattern, and introduce "implied" movement as a replacement for forced movement.

CHAPTER 4

Implied mobility

4.1 Objective

We are motivated to replace the concept of forced mobility with a concept of implied mobility (to be described shortly) for the following reasons:

(1) We wish to be able to say something about the impact of distributional change upon specific mobility routes. It would be desirable to allocate "forced cases", under some scheme, to the various routes.

(2) We wish to enlarge upon the concept of "circulatory" mobility by viewing it as a fundamental pattern rather than as merely a residual. We shall argue that it is more plausible to suppose that the observed mobility pattern is a *modification* of the circulatory pattern due to structural factors than it is to suppose that the circulatory pattern is secondary, a *residual* of the observed pattern, as in Kahl's (1957) scheme.

4.2 The elementary case

Analysis here is based on the crude mobility table introduced previously. The defects of this format will be temporarily ignored. The intended value of the present discussion is primarily in an elementary presentation of a technique which can be applied later to a format which may overcome the confounding effects ignored here.

Usually the origin and destination vectors (n^0, given by the row marginals and n^1, given by the column marginals) differ considerably, as seen earlier by the index $\Delta(n^0, n^1)$. We have seen empirically that this is primarily due to population changes in the occupational distribution over time, although differential fertility is also a factor. If n^0 and n^1 did not differ then the two factors would have compensated one another entirely and no movement would have been forced, but it would be unreasonable to conclude that no movement would have occurred. It is likely that, given the values and opportunities of industrialized societies, mobility would still occur.

We seek to relate the observed table to a "stable" mobility table, representing the circulatory pattern, with the same marginals n^0 at t_0 as are found in the observed table but with these same marginals (n^0) at t_1 as well. To be specific, suppose that class j has increased in the observed table. We interpret this as an increase in the recruitment by that class from other classes, relative to the recruitment rates which would have maintained class j at the original level. The amount of increase is not immediately calculable, for simultaneously with this increase in recruitment, the out-flow rates from class j may have undergone adjustment.

It seems reasonable to proceed as follows. Designate the frequencies in the hypothetical "stable" table by v_{ij}, with $n_{i.} = v_{i.} = v_{.i}$ for $i = 1, 2, \ldots, J$. First assume that for any class j there exists a number ℓ_j such that $n_{ij} = v_{ij}\ell_j$ for all classes i, $i = 1, 2, \ldots, J$. That is, in order to effect the increase in class j, all frequencies of mobility into j in the "stable" table were multiplied by a factor ℓ_j. The relative size of the contributions from classes $1, 2, \ldots, J$ into class j has been unchanged but all contributions have been altered by a single multiplier.

However, this assumption is not adequate as stated, for when the columns of the "stable" table are multiplied by $\ell_1, \ell_2, \ldots, \ell_J$, respectively, in order to match the column distribution observed at t_1, we have altered the row marginals. Hence we revise the assumption so that for any cell (i, j) the relationship between n_{ij} and v_{ij} is given by $n_{ij} = k_i v_{ij}\ell_j$. The numbers $\ell_1, \ell_2, \ldots, \ell_J$ are the destination-specific adjustment factors by which stable in-flow or recruitment rates are altered to give the new, observed marginals; the numbers $k_1, k_2, \ldots, k_J$, are corrective multipliers which assure that the row marginals in the "stable" and observed tables do, in fact, match.

An alternative approach would take a "supply" rather than recruitment perspective and would begin with the numbers $k_1, \ldots, k_J$. These could be interpreted as origin-specific adjustment factors by which stable out-flow or supply rates are altered to give the new, observed marginals and the numbers $\ell_1, \ldots, \ell_J$ would then be the corrective multipliers.

It can be shown that a mobility table uniquely implies its associated "stable" table in this model, and the k_i's and ℓ_j's can be determined within an arbitrary multiplicative constant. The method of finding the "stable" table will be elaborated and examples will be given.

We have required that $v_{i.} = v_{.i} = n_{i.}$, and that $n_{ij} = k_i v_{ij} \ell_j$. Hence

$$n_{i.} = v_{i.} = \Sigma_j v_{ij} = \Sigma_j \ (n_{ij}/k_i \ell_j) = (1/k_i) \ \Sigma \ (n_{ij}/\ell_j),$$

or

(1) $1/k_i = n_{i.}/\Sigma_j(n_{ij}(1/\ell_j))$

Also,

$$n_{j.} = v_{.j} = \Sigma_i v_{ij} = \Sigma_i(n_{ij}/k_i \ell_j) = (1/\ell_j) \ \Sigma_i(n_{ij}/k_i), \ .$$

or

(2) $1/\ell_j = n_{j.}/\Sigma_i(n_{ij}(1/k_i))$.

Interest in the k_i's and ℓ_j's is only indirect, but their calculation precedes calculation of the v_{ij}'s. An iterative approach is taken. Estimates $\ell_1^{(1)} = \ell_2^{(1)} = \ldots = \ell_J^{(1)} = 1$ are used to obtain $k_1^{(1)} = k_2^{(1)} = \ldots = k_j^{(1)}$ in (1). Then the latter set is substituted in (2) to obtain $\ell_1^{(2)}, \ldots, \ell_J^{(2)}$, and the cycling procedure is continued until convergence. The arbitrariness of the multiplier within a constant permits us to fix one, say ℓ_1, at the value 1 for all iterations.

The adjustment procedure described above is identical to a technique associated with Deming and Stephan (see Deming, 1943). For a description of its mathematical properties and various applications, see articles by Fienberg (1970a, b).

We can relate the "forced" movement of Chapter 2 to these "implied" rates as follows. Define

$$P_j = \frac{n_{.j} - n_{j.}}{n_{j.}}$$

If $n_{.j} > n_{j.}$, i.e., if class j occurs more often as a destination than as an origin, then P_j is the relative increase in j due to persons *forced into* j. If $n_{.j} < n_{j.}$, then P_j is the relative decrease in j due to persons *forced out of* j.

Next define

$$P_{ij} = \frac{n_{ij} - v_{ij}}{v_{ij}} .$$

If $n_{ij} > v_{ij}$, i.e., if route (i, j) occurs more often than in the circulatory table, then P_{ij} is the increase in this route relative to the stable frequency. That is, P_{ij} is the relative *increase* in (i, j) *implied* by distributional change. Similarly, if $n_{ij} < v_{ij}$, then P_{ij} is the relative *decrease* in (i, j) *implied* by the changed demand.

Recalling that $n_{ij} = k_i \ell_j v_{ij}$, note that $P_{ij} = (n_{ij}/v_{ij}) - 1 = k_i \ell_j - 1$, so that the array $|P_{ij}|$ summarizes the impact of the row and column adjustment factors on each cell (i, j).

It is easily shown that $\Sigma_j P_j n_{j.} = 0$ and that $\Sigma_j P_{ij} v_{ij} = 0$. We can also show that each P_j is a weighted sum of P_{ij}'s. That is,

$$\Sigma_i P_{ij} v_{ij} = \Sigma_i (n_{ij} - v_{ij}) = n_{.j} - v_{.j} = n_{.j} - n_{j.} = n_{j.} P_j = v_{j.} P_j,$$

since $n_{j.} = v_{j.} = v_{.j}$.

Therefore

$$P_j = \Sigma_i P_{ij} (v_{ij}/v_{j.}) \text{ with } \Sigma_j (v_{ij}/v_{j.}) = 1.$$

TABLE 9.

Values of P_j (bottom row) and P_{ij} for the British mobility table (Table 1).

Category of father	Category of Respondent				
	1	2	3	4	5
1	− 0.0247	− 0.0719	0.0019	0.3896	0.1781
2	− 0.0480	− 0.0942	− 0.0222	0.3562	0.1499
3	− 0.0788	− 0.1234	− 0.0537	0.3125	0.1128
4	− 0.1257	− 0.1680	− 0.1019	0.2456	0.0561
5	− 0.1227	− 0.1652	− 0.0988	0.2499	0.0597
	− 0.0513	− 0.1139	− 0.0536	0.2948	0.0956

Table 9 shows the values of P_{ij} and P_j for the previously discussed British table.

The proportions of forced movement, $|P_j|$, are greatest into category 4 and greatest out of category 2. Looking at the array $|P_{ij}|$, we see that for categories dominated by out-movement, viz. 1, 2, and 3, the mobility routes most affected (as proportions, not frequencies) are (4, 1), (4, 2), and (4, 3), respectively. That is, the category (4) into which movement is greatest happens also to be the one of (relatively) greatest out-movement from categories 1, 2, and 3. For categories dominated by in-movement, viz. 4 and 5, the routes most affected are (1, 4) and (1, 5), and only secondarily (2, 4) and (2, 5). Category 2, the dominant over-all "feeder" category, is a major supplier to categories 4 and 5, but it is exceeded (in relative terms) by category 1 as a supplier to 4 and 5. The complementarity in (a) above need not hold; the interior of Table 9 is not just a different form for the set $|P_j|$.

From the $|P_{ij}|$ we see that certain routes, including each of those in category 4, experienced considerable expansion of one-quarter and more, whereas certain routes such as (1, 3), changed very little as a result of distributional change.

The main diagonal routes, those of strict inheritance, were among those that were only slightly affected, except for inheritance of stratum 4, which was much greater than it otherwise would have been.

There is no particular tendency for extreme distance routes to be altered more or less than short distance routes, although inspection of the table might spuriously indicate otherwise. The procedure used to obtain the sets $|k_i|$ and $|\ell_j|$ is invariant under permutations of rows (and columns), and does not depend upon any ordinality of strata.

4.3 The role of differential fertility

As before, in order to use the crude inter-generational table, we must assume that the fathers represent a point in time that is one "generation" earlier than the date of the sample.

We shall retain the convention of Chapter 4 that fathers are fixed at time 0, sons at time 1. Two different conceptualizations will be described, with the same results.

First, when sons were sampled at time 1, we obtained a *weighted* sample of fathers at time 0; because of differential fertility of fathers, a given son may represent one father, half a father (if the father had two sons), etc. Fathers in a category i for which R_i is relatively large will be oversampled, etc. and the distribution of fathers at time 0, and hence of the labor force at time 0, will simply be the vector $|n_{i.}/R_i|$. Define $N = \Sigma_i n_{i.}$ and $q = (1/N) \Sigma(n_{i.}/R_i)$. Then the vector $1/q|n_{i.}/R_i|$ will add to N, the total in the original vector. Call this new vector X. If the observed table is adjusted to have X as both origin and destination distributions, then this adjusted table will describe the mobility patterns that would have obtained had their been *neither* differential fertility nor distributional change, as indicated by the earlier discussion. That is, this pattern is "controlled" for *both* components.

The above paragraph applies if we have a mobility table and the category-specific net reproduction rates of the fathers, $|R_i|$. If, instead of the $|R_i|$, we have the distribution of the actual labor force at approximately time 0, then we need simply to think of preserving this distribution. But this distribution is what was called m^0 in Chapter 3, and since we noted there that $n_i^0 = R_i m_i^0$, that is, $m_i^0 = n_i^0/R_i$, we see that m^0 and X are the same vector. By adjusting the observed table to have origin and destination vector m^0, we have simply incorporated the $|R_i|$ into the adjustment factors for rows. We shall henceforth drop the notation, X, and shall use the earlier referrent, m^0.

Let $T(n^0, n^1)$ represent the observed table, $T(n^0. n^0)$ the table developed in 4.2, and $T(m^0, m^0)$ the table suggested above. Here the arguments are the origin (row) and destination (column) distributions of T, and the tables are understood to be adjusted versions of $T(n^0, n^1)$.

$T(n^0, n^0)$ was termed the "elementary" case because it requires no information beyond the given table. It was generated on the assumption that fathers would replace themselves, and ignored differential fertility. That is, the assumptions were

(1) there is *no change* in the occupational distribution over time, and

(2) there *is* differential fertility, but of an unknown and unincorporated amount.

On the other hand, $T(m^0, m^0)$ incorporates information on fertility that was not available above, and is based on assumptions that

(1) there is *no change* in the occupational distribution over time, and

(2) there is *no* differential fertility, that is, any observable variation in fertility over classes has been recognized and removed.

CHAPTER 5

Multiplicative models and means of evaluating them

5.1 Introduction

Since the late 1960's major advancements have been made in methods for analyzing cross-classified data. These new methods have particular promise for the social sciences, since a great many sociological variables are intrinsically categorical in nature. By far the most powerful methods, such as regression and factor analysis, are limited in application to interval-level variables, and until recently very little could be done with categorical variables as such.

These new models can be described in two equivalent forms. In the first of these, the probability that an individual will have a particular combination of identifications on the respective variables is expressed as the product of quantities which are specific for the separate categories and for structural aspects of the cross-classification. The simplest interesting case, that of independence, was illustrated in Chapter 1. For that model, the probability of being in row i and column j is the product of two numbers a_i and b_j. The a_i's and b_j's can be defined as marginal probabilities if the respective sets are standardized to add to unity. In more complicated models, the sets of factors do not usually have probabilistic interpretations. The additional factors can be associated with the diagonals of the table, location below, on, or above the main diagonal, etc. (See Goodman, 1970). These structural factors can then be estimated through interative procedures. Alternatively, additional factors can be specified in advance to be, say, either zero or unity, depending on the location of cell (i, j) in the cross-classification. This special case, quasi-independence, is the one we shall intensively consider in the rest of this monograph.

An equivalent form for these models, and the one which is already more common, decomposes the logarithm of a cell frequency into additive components which are specific to rows, columns, diagonals, etc. These models have been developed by such persons as Goodman (1971a) and Haberman (1974) and several programs for their application are now available.

Quasi-independence, the simplest extension of the model of statistical independence, is termed quasi-perfect mobility in application to mobility data. Its parameters are the easiest to estimate and to interpret of all the extensions. Its plausibility, which we now begin to judge in detail, hinges crucially on the choice of cells which are constrained to zero. The next section considers what kinds of constraints are reasonable on a purely structural, non-empirical basis.

5.2 Quasi-perfect mobility: choice of blocked routes

To define valid blocking we must look for some variable which is likely to partition the population into parts which inherit or disinherit strata independently of other parts and are governed by their own supply and demand effects.

In terms of regression analysis, we seek likely co-variates, but we are limited to the information contained in the basic table. An alternative statement is that we seek to partition the interactions or degrees of freedom into separate groups.

Observe also that a given quasi-independent model is governed not only by the blocking of certain cells, but by the marginals of the *unblocked* cells as well. If the model holds, then the supply of men entering certain routes is allocated randomly to the jobs with which these routes terminate at the second time point. The supply and demand are defined by the marginals of the unblocked cells. We may readily accept constraints on the marginal totals of the entire population (or sample), but we should hesitate to accept constraints on the marginals of any arbitrary sub-population.

We can logically organize blockings into four basic types: (1) all routes with origin i are blocked out; (2) all routes with destination j are blocked out; (3) all routes in which $i - j$ takes on certain values are blocked out; (4) certain individual cells are blocked out. All *possible* blockings are some combination of these four types (of course, the first three are ultimately based on the fourth type), but certain combinations are not sensible in our context.

Consider types (1) and (2), for example. There may, indeed, be reason to believe that a particular category or group of categories operates with distinctive supply and demand parameters. The farm category appears qualitatively different in recent Western history because it involves skills (and land) which are difficult to acquire without a farm background, because farm birth rates are outstandingly high, and because there is so much movement away from farm to rural non-farm and urban areas. Similarly, for some societies inherited wealth is an important component of membership in the highest strata. Quasi-independence is not so likely to hold for such strata, and by holding them out we may be able to observe a high level of quasi-independence in the other strata. A third example is provided by the lowest stratum. If a "culture of poverty" exists by which movement out of the lowest stratum is particularly difficult, then one can reasonably block out this stratum. However, blocking of types (1) and (2) would be harder to motivate for strata of intermediate status.

Ideally, one would only block entire rows or columns because of prior reasoning, and not after examination of the data. Blocking after examination of relative departures from, say, the full model of independence, will be subject to randomness in the sample, and to the way in which relative errors (and estimated expected frequencies) are dependent on more than the row and column in which they appear. (For example, in Chapter 7 we will note that in small tables, the cells with smallest frequencies tend to have the largest relative errors.)

The prior reasons which lead one to block a certain row or column will usually, I believe, lead to blocking *both* the row and column associated with a given occupational group. One may be able to give good reasons why, for example, movement *into* farm categories is particularly non-random, or why movement *out* of the lowest stratum is particularly non-random. But it is likely that both in- and out-movement will be mitigated by the same stratum-related factors.

Consider now blockings of type (3), in which the difference $i - j$ takes on integral values. Any interest in such differences for values other than $i - j = 0$ implies ordinality and, in fact, interval scaling of the categories. Although we may order three strata 1, 2, 3, we can rarely assume that the increment in prestige, or whatever, from 3 to 2 is equal to that from 2 to 1. If we could assume this, we could also employ more powerful analytic techniques and would not even be thinking in terms of contingency tables. Thus

50

we do not have strong reasons for grouping together routes (3, 2) and (2, 1), the routes such that $i - j = 1$ in a 3×3 table.

If a researcher wishes to block out routes of "far movement" in which the differences $i - j$ and $j - i$ are large, he must recognize the arbitrariness of defining such routes by, say, $i - j \geqslant 3$ in a five stratum system. Such a blocking may retain some routes which, in fact, involve more "distance" in prestige and income, say, than some routes which are held out. For large tables, such as the 17×17 U.S. mobility table of Chapter 6, even detailed ordinality of strata is questionable.

The one exception to the poor definition of "far movement" is the trivial one in which we block the two cells of maximum movement, i.e., those for which $|i - j| = J - 1$ in a J-stratum table. If ordinality holds, then these two cells uniquely define the most extreme movement, and it is not necessary to assume that an equal interval scale obtains. For a small number of strata, e.g., three or four, such a blocking would be of interest. For a large number of strata, the number of persons who appear in these two corner cells will be so small that this blocking would have a trivial effect, as well as being somewhat arbitrary.

Similarly, routes of "near movement," in which $i - j$ assumes small non-zero values, are subject to the same limitations as those of "far-movement" so far as blockings are concerned.

The strict mover-stayer definition leads to a blocking of the main diagonal, on which $i - j = 0$, and makes no requirement of ordinality. Assuming that some ordinality, at least, exists in definitions of categories, Appendix 4 gives purely technical reasons why the diagonal blocking must be modified so that at most one stratum appears in *both* the upward and downward portions of the table. In a 5×5 table, for example, the minimum "stayer" blocking is thus that of Chapter 1.

An efficient way of (a) employing the ordinality of the strata definitions, (b) overcoming the technical limitations described in Appendix 4, and (c) not implying an underlying interval scale, is by joint use of the model in which only cells with $i - j > 0$ are *not* blocked and the model in which only cells with $i - j < 0$ are *not* blocked. Here we partition persons according as they have been downwardly or upwardly mobile. This basic mobility behavior is an indicator of a whole constellation of characteristics of competition, talent, aspiration, etc., relating origin and destination, and seems a valid basis for stratifying both the population and the marginals of the table.

We must slightly alter the definitions of the triangular blockings as follows. If all cells on and below the diagonal are constrained, so that only the cells of downward mobility are to be fitted, then necessarily two cells in the upper triangle will be determined by the adjusted marginals. In a J x J table, cells (1, 2) and (J − 1, J) will be the only cells in their column and row, respectively, which are not fitted: however, since these column and row totals are con-strained, these cell frequencies will be uniquely determined. Similarly for the triangle of upward mobility.

Each triangle will have $(J − 2)(J − 3)/2$ degrees of freedom, as can be verified by induction. We can reconstruct the mobile popu-lation concept for the cells (1, 2), (2, 1), (J − 1, J), and (J, J − 1) by combining the expectations in these triangles with a total of $(J − 2)(J − 3)$ degrees of freedom. In this way we can make a pooled evaluation or test of the model with nearly as many degrees of freedom as in the simple mover-stayer bifurcation with $(J − 1)^2 − J$, falling short of that number by only $2J − 5$ degrees of freedom.

Earlier it was noted that certain blockings were partially invali-dated by arbitrary definitions of categories. To an extent *all* block-ings must suffer from this problem, including the preceding three blockings. Every application involves combining occupations into groups, and the breadth of horizontal mobility distance within each stratum is just as variable and indeterminate as the vertical distance between categories discussed earlier. At best we can try to define all strata equally broadly. Avoidance of single categories with very small origin and/or destination totals will ameliorate the problem.

Finally, we observe that blockings of type (4) require particu-larly careful justification. When White first applied the model (1963) he held out cells (1, 1) and (3, 3) in a 3 x 3 table; that is, he assumed a random allocation of men to jobs for all persons who did not inherit their father's stratum *and* were not in the highest and lowest strata. Without evidence that inheritance in these cate-gories is qualitatively different from inheritance in other cate-gories, and in view of the dominant role played by the largely arbitrary definitions of categories, we discourage such constraints. Other isolated cells (except those of extreme movement, already mentioned) appear even less likely to be defensible in mobility applications. (In some contexts, such as attitude change, it is quite conceivable that certain specific routes of attitude change would be unlikely, by reason of logical inconsistency or cognitive dissonance, so that the constraint of those routes to zero would be sensible.)

The blockings we shall employ herein are (a) the null blocking, i.e., the simple model of independence, (b) the minimal stayer blocking, (c) upward and downward mover blockings; these shall sometimes be combined with (d) deletion of the farm category. Some less interpretable blockings were experimented with, but results will not be presented for them.

5.3 Interpretation of the model

We do not expect any model to predict mobility frequencies with great accuracy; our main goal is to learn *how much* movement it does account for. That is, with a suitable partitioning of the population, how much movement is accounted for by origin and destination effects alone? The question is, "how *well* does this model do", and we shall soon indicate how the evaluation differs from the testing of a hypothesis.

But if the model did hold true for a set of data, what would be the interpretation? We can simply re-phrase the comments in Chapter 1. Quasi-independence means multiplicative origin and destination effects, conditional upon some characteristic of the sub-population, such as upward mobility. If the model holds, then for all persons with this characteristic, the probability of any specific destination is a constant, given their origin, and vice versa. It is, say, equally "easy", in terms of probabilities, for a person from category 2 to move into category 3 as it is to move into category 4. Predispositions are non-existent, and ascriptive features (earlier or father's occupation, in particular) have no role in determining future occupation. Thus, the characteristic for which we controlled in the partitioning "explains" the ordinal ranking, in the sense that by conditioning on the partitioning characteristic, we eliminate the effect of the distance hierarchy between categories implied by the ordinal ranking. In other words, the ranking system has no impact other than permitting us to form homogeneous groups such as downward movers, stayers, and upward movers; this apparent by-product of the ranking system is, in fact, its essence, if the model is correct.

Any further elaboration must just be a repetition of the above points: the partitioned groups are homogeneous with respect to opportunities, and ascribed characteristics have no net effect, given that a person has moved upwards, etc.

5.4 Measures for evaluating quasi-independence

Several measures can tell us how well the model fits. Some of these, though computed, are not reported in the later chapters because they failed to discriminate well or are less interpretable.

Say that n_{ij} is the observed frequency and ν_{ij} is the expected frequency in cell (i, j). Then, excluding the measure of Section 5.7, we have the following indices:

(I) For each cell (i, j), the relative error of the observation, relative to the expectation,

$$e_{ij} = (n_{ij} - \nu_{ij})/\nu_{ij} \ .$$

(II) For each value of $k = |i - j|$, $k = 0, \ 1, \ 2, \ldots, \ J - 1$, the average relative errors

$$e_k = (1/t_k) \Sigma_{i,j} e_{ij}$$

and

$$e_k' = (1/t_k) \Sigma_{i,j} |e_{ij}| \ ,$$

where in each case the summation is over i and j such that $|i - j| = k$ and such that (i, j) is not blocked. t_k is the number of unblocked cells for each value of k.

These elementary measures indicate the degree of departure from the model with weights equal to the reciprocal of the expectation. They are computed in full recognition that we have only an ordering of the strata and not an equal interval scale.

(III) For the table as a whole,

A.   The overall average relative error,

$$e = (1/t) \Sigma_{i,j} e_{ij}$$

where the summation extends over all unblocked cells (i, j) and where t is the number of such cells.

B.   The chi-square statistic,

$$X^2 = \Sigma_{i,j} [(n_{ij} - \nu_{ij})^2 / \nu_{ij}] = \Sigma_{i,j} e_{ij} (n_{ij} - \nu_{ij}) = \Sigma_{i,j} e_{ij}^2 \nu_{ij} \ ,$$

where the summation extends over all unblocked cells. If B is the number of *blocked* cells which are linearly independent of (i.e., not determined by the marginals in a J x J table, then X^2 is asymptotically distributed as χ^2 with $(J-1)^2 - B$ degrees of freedom.

X^2 can be used to *test* the null hypothesis of quasi-independence in a table, but it is in no way a measure of association and cannot be used to describe how well the model fits, other than to say that it does or does not fit. (See, for example, Goodman and Kruskal, 1954.) Several attempts have been made to normalize X^2, however, to adapt it to non-testing situations. Two of these follow.

C. *The phi-square coefficient,*

$$\phi^2 = X^2/N ,$$

where N is the unblocked total frequency. Given an alternative probability distribution which differs from that of the null hypothesis, X^2 will increase asymptotically in proportion to N, so ϕ^2 takes out the main effect of the sample size. It is ordinarily applied to 2 x 2 tables, but need not be so restricted.

We can relate ϕ^2 to an informational measure, which we can call $I(\theta)$, as follows. (For another sociological use of $I(\theta)$, see Theil and Finizza, 1971.) Suppose we are given an observed set $|p_k|$ and a theoretical set $|\theta_k|$ of proportions over J categories. The expected value of the information required to transform the observed set into the theoretical set, i.e., a measure of the distance from the theoretical set, is

$$I(\theta) = -\Sigma_k \theta_k \log(p_k/\theta_k) .$$

The base of the logarithms here is arbitrary; we shall assume natural logarithms (base e) are used.

Note that

$$\log(p_k/\theta_k) = \log(1 + (p_k - \theta_k)/\theta_k) = \log(1 + x_k),$$

if we define $x_k = (p_k - \theta_k)/\theta_k$. The first two terms of the Taylor series expansion for $\log(1 + x)$ are $\log(1 + x) \doteq x - (x^2/2)$.

The truncated series gives a good approximation if x is small relative to unity. Then

$$I(\theta) \doteq -\Sigma_k [(\theta_k (p_k - \theta_k)/\theta_k) - (\theta_k/2)((p_k - \theta_k)/\theta_k)^2]$$

$$= -\Sigma_k p_k + \Sigma_k \theta_k + \tfrac{1}{2}\Sigma_k [(p_k - \theta_k)^2/\theta_k]$$

$$= -1 + 1 + \tfrac{1}{2}(X^2/N) = \phi^2/2 .$$

Thus, for small relative errors the computed ϕ^2 will be closely proportional to the informational measure $I(\theta)$, which has an interpretation independent of X^2.

Note that $I(\theta)$ is defined far differently from the informational measure I in Chapter 1. I measures departure from a uniform distribution, but $I(\theta)$ can measure departure from any theoretical distribution.

D.   *The coefficient of contingency,*

$$C = [\phi^2/(\phi^2 + 1)]^{\tfrac{1}{2}} = [X^2/(X^2 + N)]^{\tfrac{1}{2}}$$

The intention behind this well-known coefficient is the normalization of the range of X^2. Clearly, C must be less than one; equally clearly, it cannot attain one.

Other normalization attempts have been made; for example, Cramer's coefficient takes into account the number of degrees of freedom of the table. However, Cramer's procedure cannot be directly extended to tables with constrained cells, and because of the basic shortcomings of X^2-based measures, this extension has not been utilized.

E.   *Modified gamma.*

This measure and the next were especially developed for the measurement of association between two categorical variables when certain cells are constrained to zero. Gamma was developed by Goodman and Kruskal (1954) as a measure of association when the two variables are ordinal (and no cells are constrained). It has a clear interpretation as measuring the proportionate reduction in error in the prediction of one of the variables that results from knowing the value taken by the other variable. (See also Costner, 1965.) It is symmetric with respect to the two variables, and has a range in the interval [−1, 1]. Regardless of the marginals of the ordinary two-way table, the observations *can* fall in such a way that either extreme value is attained. The sampling theory of gamma is known and one can test for a specified level of association (Goodman and Kruskal, 1963).

When certain cells are constrained, however, problems arise. We can readily compute gamma for the observed table; but if certain cells are constrained, then it is not reasonable to include those cells in the computation; our question is, "how much association exists between origin and distribution when the blocked cells have been removed?" The first way one might consider handling the constrained cells would be by replacing their observed frequencies with zeroes. However, the computation of gamma is in terms of pairs of observations lying in different cells of the table, and by deleting all observations in constrained cells we exclude large numbers of pairs, altering drastically the value of gamma.

It is well known that if statistical independence maintains in an ordinary table, then gamma takes the value zero. The most reasonable way to develop a modified gamma would be to require that (1) it be zero when quasi-independence maintains over the unblocked cells of a table, and (2) the blocked cells be assigned adjusted frequencies such that (1) holds, but otherwise the computation and interpretation of the modified gamma should be identical with those of gamma.

It is a simple matter to meet these conditions. If quasi-independence holds in a table then each unblocked frequency can be expressed as the product of origin-specific and destination-specific factors. If the blocked cells are then "fitted" with adjusted frequencies equal to the product of the origin factor and destination factor computed for the *un*blocked cells with the corresponding origin and destination, and if the usual gamma computed for this partially adjusted table *differs* from zero, then gamma will measure the association due to the unadjusted, i.e., unblocked cells, as desired.

Consequently, the modified gamma is defined by two steps: (1) "reconstruct" the blocked frequencies using the origin and destination factors computed over unblocked cells, and (2) compute the usual gamma. To the extent that the modified gamma differs from zero, there is association between origin and destination over the unconstrained mobility routes.

The modified gamma was computed for all tables discussed later herein, but its interpretability is much hampered by its unstandardized range. As noted before, the range of the ordinary gamma does not depend on the marginal distributions; we can always fill in the interior of the table to attain the extreme values of gamma. In the present case, however, when part of the *interior* of the table is constrained, the limits -1 and $+1$ may not be attainable. In particular, when we require that there be a large number of persons (movers) off the main diagonal, then the upper limit of gamma is considerably lowered, since perfect association ($\gamma = 1$) requires that all (or nearly all) of the cases lie on the main diagonal in a square table.

Ideally, one would make the further adjustment to the modified gamma of correcting for its range using corrected limits. That is, if

γ = observed gamma (modified)

γ_{min} = minimum gamma possible with given constraints

γ_{max} = maximum gamma possible with given constraints

γ_A = γ adjusted for range

then (keeping in mind that $\gamma = 0$ still means complete lack of association) we could define

$$\gamma_A = \begin{cases} \gamma/\gamma_{min} & \text{if} \quad \gamma \leqslant 0 \\ \gamma/\gamma_{max} & \text{if} \quad \gamma > 0 \end{cases}$$

Or, if we require a function with a continuous first derivative we could define

$$\gamma_A = [(2\gamma - (\gamma_{max} + \gamma_{min}))/(\gamma_{max} - \gamma_{min})]$$

Of course, this definition would not have $\gamma_A = 0$ when $\gamma = 0$, and my preference would therefore be for the first definition of γ_A.

A little experimentation will reveal that it is difficult to compute the limiting values of gamma when cells are constrained; in fact, the very meaning of association when diagonal cells are constrained is obscure. The range seems to be sensitive to the choice of blocking, but because no general way has been found for computing γ_{max} and γ_{min}, we are left with only the unstandardized but modified γ. We hesitate to make much use of the uniformly small values obtained because the blockings themselves have forced gamma to be small.

58

F. Modified lambda.

Lambda was developed by Goodman and Kruskal (1954) as a measure of association when two categorical variables are only nominal in level of measurement. It has the same probabilistic, reduction-of-error interpretations as gamma, but it is defined asymetrically, under the assumption that one variable precedes the other. Such an assumption is entirely appropriate for mobility, although if our occupational classifications are in fact ordinal, then lambda makes use of less information than does gamma.

We shall simply note that if the hypothesis of quasi-independence is satisfied in a table, then if that table is modified as above through the use of origin and destination factors to "reconstruct" frequencies in constrained cells, then a lambda computed for the full table will take the value zero. Lambda ordinarily has a range [0, 1], but, as with gamma, cell constraints severely limit the range of lambda. Although I believe it would be easier to determine the range of lambda than that of gamma, this direction was not explored. A major reason was that computations of the modified lambda (computed on the same table as the modified gamma) gave extremely small values, quite often zero. Thus it appeared unlikely that even an adjustment for range would yield a measure that could meaningfully discriminate. A less important reason was that lambda is less widely used, and a refinement would have less chance for application outside the present study.

5.5 Evaluating the model (continued): the index of dissimilarity

We wish to evaluate (rather than test) a model which imposes certain constraints on cross-classified data, and for this purpose we seek a coefficient which (1) is easily interpretable and (2) incorporates the constraints of the model. The premise is that if expectations are made subject to constraints, then these should alter our measure — in a sense similar to which degrees of freedom determine appropriate critical regions when a χ^2 test is made.

The preferred measure in our situation would be the modified gamma described in Section 5.4, because it is interpretable and takes the value zero when quasi-independence holds. Gamma was, moreover, developed for ordinal classifications. However, as reported in Section 5.4, it proved impossible to compute the range of the modified gammas, and comparisons between observed values were not useful. A low value of gamma is not good evidence of low association in the unconstrained cells if our constraints alone prevented gamma from being larger than 0.1, say, as frequently happens.

Attention has turned to a fairly commonplace (but easily interpretable) measure, the index of dissimilarity, which we shall refer to as Δ (delta). Suppose we have a pair of points x and y in a K-dimensional Euclidean space, with coordinates $x = (x_1, x_2, \ldots, x_K)$ and $y = (y_1, y_2, \ldots, y_K)$. A whole class of distance metrics, Minkowski s-metrics, is defined by the form

$$d_s(x, y) = [\Sigma_{k=1}^{K}|x_k - y_k|^s]^{1/s}.$$

If $s = 2$ then we obtain the familiar Euclidean metric, but any $s \geq 1$ will satisfy the requirements of a metric, namely (a) that distances be non-negative, (b) that the distance from x to y equals the distance from y to x, (c) that the distance from x to x is zero, and (d) that the distance from x to y plus that from y to z is not less than the direct distance from x to z. Suppose that the values on the coordinates are determined by frequencies in cross-tabulations, so that a table with K cells defines a point in K-dimensional space (we need not restrict ourselves to two-way tables). If, with the same pair-wise definitions of cells for two arrays with K cells each, we call the frequencies x_1 and y_1, x_2 and y_2, ..., x_k and y_k, with the assumption that $\Sigma x_k = \Sigma y_k = N$, then $d_s(x, y)$ given above measures the "distance" between the two tables, measuring the extent of their differential allocation of N units. Metrics of this type do not take into account any substantive ordinality of the variables which make up the table and do not even retain any grouping according to, say, a common origin or common destination as, for example, does lambda. With such lack of grouping, "proportionate reduction of error", or "prediction" interpretations are difficult to obtain. If we take $s = 1$ then $\Delta = (1/2N)d_1 (x, y)$. And Δ, the special case, does have a very attractive interpretation.

Retain for a moment the preceding notation for two sets of K numbers, $|x_k|$ and $|y_k|$, with the same frequency N in each set. Let S^+ be the set of cells in which $x_k > y_k$, and let S^- be the remaining cells, in which $x_k \leq y_k$. Note that

$$\Sigma_{S^+}|x_k - y_k| - \Sigma_{S^-}|x_k - y_k| = \Sigma_{k=1}^{K}x_k - \Sigma_{k=1}^{K}x_k = N - N = 0 ,$$

so that

60

$$\Sigma_{S^+} |x_k - y_k| = \Sigma_{S^-} |x_k - y_k| = \tfrac{1}{2}\Sigma_{k=1}^{K} |x_k - y_k| = N\Delta .$$

Thus, by shifting $N\Delta$ cases *out of* cells in S^+ and in the first array and *into* cells in S^- and in the first array we can establish equality of the $|x_k|$ and $|y_k|$ arrays. Δ itself is the *proportion* of cases which must be shifted in either array to equalize the two arrays. If one of these arrays consisted of *observed* frequencies, and the other of *expected* frequencies under some model, then $1 - \Delta$ would be the proportion of cases correctly assigned by the model, and Δ would be the proportion assigned incorrectly.

We shall, herein, interpret $1 - \Delta$ and Δ as the proportion of observations "explained" and "unexplained", respectively, by a particular model. With these terms we make an analogy (with their frequent application in regression analysis) to the proportions R^2 (the multiple correlation coefficient) and $1 - R^2$.

The analogy is weak, to be sure. R^2 tells the researcher what proportion of the variation (sum of squares) about the mean value on one continuous variable is reduced when we condition upon the values of one or more other variables in some way. $1 - \Delta$ tells what proportion of the frequencies are correctly (in the sense of matching the observations) allocated to a set of categories by a particular model.

In regression, the mean of the predicted values is constrained to match that of observed values, etc. With contingency tables, constraints on the total predicted frequency and on various linear combinations of predicted frequencies are commonly made. In each case, constraints are employed in two ways. First, in testing whether the model does apply, or does account for a statistically significant portion of the observed values, in the case of regression one makes an F-test using a function of R^2 and the number of constraints. *Both* the value of the computed F statistic and the critical region (i.e., which tabulated F applies) are functions of the number of constraints. In the case of contingency tables, on the other hand, a model is tested with a computed X^2, which does *not* depend on the number of degrees of freedom, although the tabulated distribution with which we compare X^2 does so depend. Moreover, X^2 is not a function of Δ, although F is a function (in part) of R^2.

Constraints are applied in a second sense, not to the test statistics, but to the measures of relation. $1 - R^2$ is sometimes adjusted by the factor $(N - 1)/(N - 1 - C)$, where N is the number of cases and C is the number of parameters to be estimated by a regression model. When C is large relative to N, the adjustment can be considerable. (The effect is to adjust $1 - R^2$ to a ratio of variance estimates, rather than a ratio of sums of squares.)

The next two sections of this chapter describe two major ways in which the index of dissimilarity can be strengthened through adjustments. We wish to retain Δ's interpretability but to compensate for constraints upon our predicted values that may originate in the marginals or in the interior of the table. The adjustments described can be applied far beyond the context of occupational mobility, particularly whenever a variety of tables need to be compared and a model evaluated.

5.6 Adjustment for degrees of freedom

The reason why the factor ½ appears in the definition of Δ is that, as described in Section 5.5, by "shifting" persons from the cells in $|x_k|$, say, in which $x_k > y_k$, we *must* transfer them to cells in which $x_k \leqslant y_k$. There is no need to count cases both as they are moved out and as they are moved in to other cells. As persons are shifted in the most economical way possible, a single transfer will reduce $d_1(x, y)$ by two units.

Consider, however. the following table. We are given an observed table (not shown) which, when divided through by N, has row marginals (½, ½). The first panel of Table 10 gives the expectations under a model (that of independence, say) which has the same marginals as the observed table, by constraint. The second panel of Table 10 gives the form of the observed table as a departure from the predicted table. Since a 2 x 2 table has only one degree of freedom with these constraints, the observed table can be expressed in terms of a single parameter, e. The departure can be summarized by $\Delta = \frac{1}{2}(e + e + e + e) = 2e$. However, there is

TABLE 10.

Predicted and observed tables with a one-parameter model.

¼	¼	½
¼	¼	½
½	½	1

¼ − e	¼ + e	½
¼ + e	¼ − e	½
½	½	1

another sense in which a smaller proportion of persons needs to be shifted to effect correspondence between the two tables. If, for example, a fraction e were added to cell (1, 1) of the observed table, then the marginal constraints would automatically force the remaining observations into correspondence with the model. Of course, we could not shift the fraction e into cell (1, 1) without simultaneously shifting them out of another cell, such as (1, 2). The process might be rephrased as, say, shifting a fraction e from (1, 2) into (1, 1) and then following through with the implied adjustments for maintenance of column totals. The essential point is that by establishing a correspondence of observations with the model in only a subset of the observed table, the total correspondence is effected. To be sure, if the model did not assume fixed marginals but only a fixed total, then more than a proportion e would have to be shifted.

We shall use the term "fundamental set" to refer to any minimal subset of cells of a table which, together with the marginals, imply all frequencies in the table. The number of cells in each fundamental set equals the degrees of freedom of the model. When one table is adjusted to another over the cells of a fundamental set, then complete equality is implied. Usually, the specific choice of fundamental set will modify the required number of shifts. One could conceivably search for the fundamental set over which the smallest number of shifts needs to be made to "force" complete correspondence. An easier method is the averaging over all fundamental sets.

Consider only rectangular, two-way tables, with r rows and c columns, constraints on all marginals but no interior constraints. Let $S_1, S_2, \ldots, S_F$ be the fundamental sets, of which there are F, say. Let n_{ij} be the observed frequency and m_{ij} be the hypothesized frequency in cell (i, j). The average proportion that must be shifted over all fundamental sets is

$$\Delta'' = (1/FN) \Sigma_{f=1}^{F} [\Sigma_{\substack{(i, j) \\ \epsilon S_f}} |n_{ij} - m_{ij}|]$$

Each fundamental set consists of $(r - 1)(c - 1)$ cells, of which no more than $r - 1$ are in any given column and no more than $c - 1$ are in any given row. If we were to list all F such sets in some fashion we would find that (due to certain structural invariance of the table under permutations of rows and columns) each cell of the table would appear in the same number of sets, say

63

G. That is, each cell in the double summation for Δ'' above appears G times, so we can write

$$\Delta' = (G/FN)\Sigma_{i=1}^{r}\Sigma_{j=1}^{c}|n_{ij} - m_{ij}| = (2G/F)\Delta$$

Later in this chapter we shall compute F exactly, but for the present we need only to evaluate the ratio G/F in terms of r and c.

As before, suppose we list all the fundamental sets. If we add up the total number of cells in this list (including the many repetitions) we will obtain $(r - 1)(c - 1)$ F cells. On the other hand, each cell in the table will have appeared G times, so that this total cell count can be expressed as rcG. That is, $(r - 1)(c - 1)F = rcG$, and $2G/F = 2(r - 1)(c - 1)/rc$, so that $\Delta'' = 2(r - 1)(c - 1)\Delta/rc$.

We immediately observe that

$$\lim_{\substack{r \to \infty \\ c \to \infty}} \Delta'' = 2\Delta$$

It is intuitively clear that if we had correctly adjusted for degrees of freedom, then as the size of the table increased, so that the number of constraints expressed as a fraction of the total cells to be fitted approached zero, then the adjusted Δ should approach the original Δ. In order to achieve this convergence as r and c become infinite, we insert a factor of ½ in the definition of Δ''. In conclusion, we define the df (degrees freedom) – adjusted Δ' by

$$\Delta' = (G/F)\Delta = (r - 1)(c - 1)\Delta/rc$$

Some values of the adjustment factor for small values of r and c are given in Table 11. For reasons of symmetry, the lower triangle is not shown. Note that if there are only two rows (or columns) then, as the number of columns (or rows) increases, the factor G/F tends toward ½ (from below).

To interpret this adjustment, suppose that we had a male-female distribution over c occupational categories, and by our model assumed that the numbers of males and females in the labor force was fixed, and the number of persons in each occupational category was fixed. Suppose we compared an observed table with the model of independence, which gives the same occupational distribution to each sex, and we computed the index of dissimilarity.

TABLE 11.

Degrees-of-freedom adjustment factors for the usual Δ in a table with r rows, c columns, and no interior restraints.

r \ c	2	3	4	5	6	10	∞
2	0.25	0.33	0.38	0.40	0.42	0.45	0.50
3		0.44	0.50	0.54	0.56	0.60	0.67
4			0.57	0.60	0.63	0.68	0.75
5				0.64	0.67	0.72	0.80
6					0.70	0.75	0.83
10						0.81	0.90
∞							1.00

Whatever value we obtained for Δ will be reduced to less than (½)Δ for the revised "minimum proportionate shift" interpretation. Our constraints *force* the remaining shift.

Note that if a given set of data is expanded by the subdivision of rows and/or columns, we will simultaneously have (a) disaggregation, (b) an increase in degrees of freedom, and (c) an increase in constraints. It is easily seen that disaggregation requires Δ to increase or to remain constant; Δ cannot decrease as a table is expanded through subdivision. Δ' does not correct Δ for aggregation-disaggregation. We have responded only to (b) and (c) above in that a smaller fraction of the crude Δ (a fraction $1 - F/G$) is considered to be a result of constraints as the number of constraints increases. It is not clear how one could correct for (a) above.

If certain cells are constrained to certain values then the table loses those invariance properties which result in the constant G, the number of times a cell appears over all fundamental sets for the case of no internal constraints. In such cases we would redefine Δ' by

$$\Delta = (1/2NF)\Sigma_{i=1}^{r}\Sigma_{j=1}^{c}g_{ij}|n_{ij} - m_{ij}|,$$

where the summation is restricted to unconstrained cells and the number g_{ij} is the number of times cell (i, j) appears over all S_f. Because of the difficulty in computing the g_{ij}, an approximate formula is

$$\Delta' = (f/K)\Delta, \text{ where}$$

65

f   = degrees of freedom of the table
K   = number of cells to be fitted.

This formula coincides with the preceding one for Δ' when no cells are constrained. It becomes less accurate as the number of cells constrained in a given row or given column increases. The order of approximation is a function of the blocking pattern.

To summarize, if we have a table of observed frequencies, and a computed table of expected frequencies, then Δ' will be the fraction of persons in the observed table who would have to be relocated to match the expected table. $1 - \Delta'$ will be the proportion who are correctly located by the model.

The unadjusted index Δ is reported in the following chapters. Most of our comparisons will be between different data sets with a fixed table size and blocking pattern, and therefore the same adjustment factor. Δ' is therefore omitted but can be readily computed from those numbers provided the reader. The large amount of data to be analyzed precludes presenting all of the measures we consider useful.

5.7 The maximum value of Δ and the measure L

The crude index Δ is subject to rather severe limits on its range, particularly when some interior cells are constrained. The lower limit is always zero, and can be attained, but the upper limit is a function of the observed table and all constraints. In this section we discuss the computation of this maximum value, called Δ_{max}.

We are given (a) an observed array or table, and (b) an array of expectations, subject to some model and some constraints, such as correspondence in marginals with the observed array. Δ, we have seen, is a measure of the distance between the two arrays, or of the amount of relocation of units inside one table that would lead to correspondence in all cells with the other table. It is symmetric in that the "distance" from table (a) to table (b) is the same as from table (b) to table (a), and the shift of cases in one table would equal the shift of cases in the other table, regardless of whether we changed (a) to match (b) or (b) to match (a).

This symmetry in form can be exploited in conceptualizing the meaning of Δ_{max}. Ordinarily, in classical statistics, one takes a set of expectations, obtained from some model, as an origin, and considers the set of observations as departures from those expectations because of some random or systematic sources of variation.

The observations are used through their row and column totals (the sufficient statistics) to generate expectations for all cells. Classically, one tests a model by evaluating how "close" the observed table is to the expected table, given the correspondence in row and column totals.

This viewpoint could certainly be employed in the present analysis, as in most statistical work, but I have chosen to reverse the orientation for the computation of Δ_{max}. This reversal is, to an extent, arbitrary, and the algorithms to be discussed in this chapter are in no way dependent on this orientation.

Let T_0 be the observed table. We shall assume that T_0 itself generates a class of tables, all with the same marginal frequencies (and possibly internal constraints) as T_0. Elements of this class, in addition to T_0, include tables generated by a range of theoretical models, as well as many tables not likely to be of theoretical interest. For example, the model of independence between the rows and columns of T_0 will generate a hypothetical table within this class (refer to the class as $C(T_0)$).

Our question is, "how well does a particular model describe a given set of data, relative to all models that have the same (or more) constraints as the particular model?" In symbols, given some procedure for computing a coefficient ξ, the observed T_0, and a theoretical $T_x \epsilon C(T_0)$, we compute the discrepancy $\xi(T_0, T_x)$. The proposal advanced here is that this ξ should be normed by

ξ_{max}, where ξ_{max} is defined to be

$$\max_{T_y \epsilon C(T_0)} \xi(T_0, T_y).$$

In classical statistics we would norm by

$$\max_{T_y \epsilon C(T_x)} \xi(T_x, T_y).$$

However, under the circumstances described above, ξ_{max} as defined is more responsive to the question we have asked. If we are going to norm our index at all, I prefer to norm it relative to alternative models than relative to alternative arrangements of data. The actual algorithm to be described, however, could be as easily used for either choice of norm.

The measure ξ used here is Δ, the index of dissimilarity, but the above orientation could apply to other measures, e.g., chi-square based measures. The reason for using Δ is that other measures are either less tractable or less interpretable.

The remainder of this section is concerned with the following maximization problem.

Given: an array of observed frequencies

$$|n_{ij}; \; i = 1, \ldots, r \text{ and } j = 1, \ldots, c| \, .$$

Problem: to find the array $|m_{ij}; i = 1, \ldots, r \text{ and } j = 1, \ldots, c|$, subject to the constraints

(a) $\Sigma_i m_{ij} = \Sigma_i n_{ij}$ for all j

(b) $\Sigma_j m_{ij} = \Sigma_j n_{ij}$ for all i

(c) $\Sigma_{i,j} m_{ij} = \Sigma_{i,j} n_{ij} = N$

(d) $m_{ij} = n_{ij} = 0$ for all (i, j) in a set of constrained cells

which maximizes

$$\Delta = (1/2N)\Sigma_{i,j}|n_{ij} - m_{ii}| \, ,$$

i.e., which maximizes

$$D = \Sigma_{i,j}|n_{ij} - m_{ij}|$$

The array $|m_{ij}|$ will be referred to as the MDT, or "most different table"; the maximum value of Δ is Δ_{max}. It may happen that more than one array $|m_{ij}|$ will produce the same index Δ_{max}, in which case any one of these arrays will serve as MDT. Our interest is in Δ_{max}, but it appears that this number can be obtained only by computation of the MDT, and an algorithm is required to yield the MDT.

In format, of course, the problem is an exercise in non-linear programming, for we wish to maximize a function of the observations with linear constraints, and the sum in D or Δ is non-linear in the $|n_{ij}|$. Non-linear programming is a rapidly developing area of applied mathematics, but to my knowledge it cannot yet handle sums of absolute differences. If we were working with a second-order Minkowski metric with terms $|n_{ii} - m_{ij}|^2 = n_{ij}^2 - 2n_{ii}m_{ij} + m_{ij}^2$ we could apply quadratic programming. Maximization is a

68

substantially more difficult programming problem with absolute values, as in D or Δ. The technique we shall use is less analytic, and for that reason we cannot give a proof that Δ_{max} is, in fact, obtained by our technique. At best, we have an excellent estimate. The true Δ_{max} may be greater (not less) than the estimate. There is good evidence that our estimates are accurate. For example, a few tables were small enough to be handled without a computer, by trial and error, so that Δ_{max} could be computed exactly. The algorithm agreed perfectly with the correct result for these tables. We feel that the gain in interpretation in the use of a norm, even if not perfectly estimated, is far preferable to using, in effect, a norm of unity when Δ cannot possibly approach unity.

The alogrithm is developed in Appendix 6. Appendix 7 gives a listing of the computer program employed. Given the computed Δ_{max}, we can compute a standardized index L defined in the next paragraph.

Let Δ be the crude index of dissimilarity. Then $1 - \Delta$ is the proportion of cases correctly located in a table. However, we have found that $1 - \Delta_{max}$ cases *had* to be located correctly simply because of the marginal constraints (and the limitation to non-negative cell frequencies). The difference, $(1 - \Delta) - (1 - \Delta_{max}) = \Delta_{max} - \Delta$, is the proportion of cases correctly located *beyond* the minimum proportion. Δ can, of course, assume a minimum of zero. Thus the quantity

$$L = (\Delta_{max} - \Delta)/(\Delta_{max} - 0) = 1 - \Delta/\Delta_{max}$$

is the standardized proportion correctly located, standardized for the range [0, 1]. Note that if Δ_{max} has been under-estimated, then L has also been under-estimated. This quantity is considered the most important evaluative index in the chapters which follow.

CHAPTER 6

Quasi-independence applied to mobility data from the United States

6.1 Data from the Six Cities Study

In the first part of this chapter we shall attempt to establish the range and variability of mobility patterns in the United States. Since the range of conditions which produce such patterns is limited in any specific country we can anticipate a narrow range of patterns. However, the extent of the variation that does exist will help us to evaluate international differences.

The data that will be used are from the United States, specifically from the "Six Cities Study", most completely described in *Labor Mobility in Six Cities*, by Gladys Palmer (1954). The data we shall present are drawn from a tape of the original data and, I believe, are not available from any previously published source. The larger study had two major motivations. First, it sought to describe the workers who changed jobs between 1940 and 1950, and the kinds of changes that were made. Second, it was an effort to test theories about the operation of the labor market. Palmer's summary of the major findings of the survey indicate the orientation:

1. Mobility is not characteristic of all members of the labor force, but is concentrated within certain of its parts.

2. Differences in the incidence of mobility among various groups of workers, and the kinds of job shifts made follow similar patterns in different cities, regardless of whether a city's mobility is relatively high or low.

3. The incidence of mobility differs at various levels of skill, but even highly stable occupational groups have mobile segments.

4. A labor force adapts more readily to changes in the

industrial demand for labor than to changes in the occupational structure.

5. Persistent intercity contrasts suggest the existence of area differentials in mobility.

6. Expanding employment in a city attracts workers from other areas, and migrants are relatively flexible in adjusting to labor market changes.

7. Workers who are experienced in certain occupations can transfer their skills to certain others, but there is a limit to the amount of interchange between levels of skill.

8. When employment is at a high level, voluntary job changes outnumber involuntary changes, and tend to reflect an improvement in economic position and in the knowledge and skills of workers (Palmer, 1954, p. 7).

The six cities studied were Philadelphia, New Haven, Chicago, St. Paul, San Francisco, and Los Angeles, and they were chosen at least as much for convenience as for other characteristics. They do illustrate a considerable range in age and geographical location, and a lesser range in size and type of economic base. The Bureau of the Census and local research centers cooperatively collected a total of 13,000 work history schedules from random samples in each city of persons twenty-five years of age and older who worked for at least one month in 1950. The data were collected in January and February of 1951. Occupational categories developed by the Bureau of the Census were used.

Of course, the persons interviewed in a given city in 1951 need not have been there during the entire decade of the study. Some may have come from other cities or from rural occupations. The latter persons were dropped for our purposes. The decade included World War II, which affected amounts of movement, particularly through the short-term mobilization of women into the labor force.

Variation in absolute levels

Variation in *patterns* of movement, as developed earlier, are superimposed upon more basic characteristics. At the first level one can evaluate the actual strength of the labor force. "Work rates" in 1951 ranged from 73 per cent in New Haven to 80 per cent in Chicago, for men aged fourteen and over, and from 29 per cent in St. Paul to 37 per cent in San Francisco for women aged fourteen and over. The ranges are reduced by only 1 per cent and

2 per cent, respectively, when the populations are standardized for age and marital status (Palmer, 1954, p. 18). At the second level one could compare occupational distributions, the marginals of Table 12, to measure disparity in occupational profiles. If some occupational scoring system were used, we could compare mean scores and dispersions. This second level is not of central interest in this work, so we shall proceed to the discussion of entire tables, the third level.

We shall compare tables simply on the basis of the degree to which they are described by various quasi-independent models. The interpretation of variations in the adequacy of these models was described in Chapter 5.

Mobility has been put within a five-class structure by deleting persons who were non-respondents for either or both of the two time points in a table, or who were outside the labor force, or who gave a farm origin or destination. We limit ourselves to white males only. The five classes used, based on the Bureau of the Census classification, are I. Professional-Managerial; II. Clerical-Sales; III. Craftsmen; IV. Operative; V. Service-Laborer.

The blockings or models used are illustrated in Figure 2. Model I is the usual model of independence, in which no cells are blocked. Model Q is the maximal quasi-independent model for ordinal data, such as we have here. The main diagonal is blocked, and in addition four cells near the diagonal are held constant so that no more than one category (viz., category III) shall be in both the upper and lower triangles of the table (see Chapter 5). Model D limits attention to downward movers only, and Model U to upward movers only. These latter two models, taken together, refer to exactly the same cells as Model Q. This characteristic holds only for 5×5 tables (not for the larger versions of the models, which will appear later herein) and is one reason why 5×5 tables were constructed. For this size of table there is a difference of only one degree of freedom between Model Q and the sum of Models D and U. That is, the sum of computed values of X^2 for the D and U models will differ from X^2 for Model Q by an amount which is distributed as χ^2 with one degree of freedom and which relates to the separation into two parts.

In general, Model I has $(J - 1)^2$ degrees of freedom; Model Q has $-1 + (J - 1)^2/2$ degrees of freedom when J, the number of categories, is odd (as it is in all our applications); Models D and U have $(J - 2)(J - 3)/2$ degrees of freedom each. Then, in general (J odd), the difference between Q and the joint U and D model has

Model I

Model Q

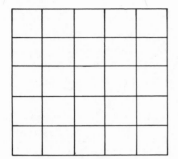

Number of free cells:	25
Degrees of freedom:	16
95%-ile of χ^2:	26.3
99%-ile of χ^2:	32.0

Number of free cells:	16
Degrees of freedom:	7
95%-ile of χ^2:	14.1
99%-ile of χ^2:	18.5

Model D

Model U

Number of free cells:	8
Degrees of freedom:	3
95%-ile of χ^2:	7.81
99%-ile of χ^2:	11.3

Number of free cells:	8
Degrees of freedom:	3
95%-ile of χ^2:	7.81
99%-ile of χ_2:	11.3

Fig. 2. The 5×5 quasi-independent models. X indicates a constrained cell.

$-[(J-4)^2 -3]/2$ degrees of freedom. (So that for odd values of J greater than 5, Models U and D jointly have *more* degrees of freedom than Model Q.)

Figure 2 also gives critical values of X^2 and, indeed, many of the tables given have smaller values of the statistic, so that these tables do not significantly oppose the relevant hypothesis of quasi-independence. But we do not attach asterisks to any of the test statistics, since testing is not our objective.

Interpretation is based on $\phi^2 = X^2/N$; e, the average absolute value of relative error; and $L = 1 - \Delta/\Delta_{max}$, the standardized proportion of cases accurately placed within a table. These quantities were defined in Sections 5.4 and 5.7. We also provide the value of the unadjusted Δ. These measures are given in Table 14. As a rule of thumb, we shall consider two values of L, where $L = 1 - \Delta/\Delta_{max}$, to be substantively (as opposed to statistically) significantly different only if their difference exceeds 0.10.*

6.2 Results for the Six Cities

The panels of Table 12 present the data for intra-generational movement in the six cities. Data were available for occupation in 1945, but so little movement occurred between 1940 and 1945 and between 1945 and 1949 that the longest possible interval, 1940–1949, was taken. Intra-generational movement from father's occupation to son's occupation in 1949 is described by the panels of Table 13. Because of a shortage of cases, it was not possible to form statistically stable tables of cohort movement within the specific cities. We did attempt some cohort analysis based on aggregation of age groups across cities. However, because the cities were selected in a non-random manner and different sampling procedures were used in each, we decided that the reference population for the pooled cohort analysis was too vague to justify discussion here.

We observe the following principal patterns in the application of the quasi-independent models of "six-city" data, using mainly Index L.

A. Within Table 12 (intra-generational movement by city):
1. The I model, simple independence, correctly locates a proportion 0.457 ± 0.035. Q correctly locates 0.815 ± 0.070. D, the model for downward moves only, locates a proportion 0.812 ± 0.058. U correctly locates a proportion 0.840 ± 0.079. We consider

---

* The author has developed approximate formulas for the standard deviation of Δ which are available from him but need not be presented here. Conservative (high) estimates indicate that differences of 0.10 are always statistically significant at a high level for these data.

the quality of fit to be very good in all cases, on the basis of the (standardized) proportion correctly located.

2. The range in quality of fit is so small that we would hesitate to relate L to any other variables in these cities, such as level of employment, sex ratio in the labor force, etc., even though these variables are available.

3. There is no apparent relation between the values of L over the I, Q, D, and U models. That the I model fits relatively well does not, for example, imply that the Q model does well in the same city. There is no tendency for the U model to do worse than the D model, or vice versa, nor for the U and D fits to be correlated.

4. The Q model refers to exactly the same cells as the D and U models, together, but it has more than the sum of their degrees of freedom. Since generally an increase in degrees of freedom means a worse fit, one might expect L to be smaller for Model Q than for Models D and U, and one might expect ϕ^2 and e to be larger for Q than for D and U. On the contrary, L, at least, tends to be *intermediate* in value for Model Q to its values on Models D and U. This pattern is an indication (more are found in Chapter 7) that L behaves as if adjusted for degrees of freedom and for aggregation.

B. Within Table 13 (inter-generational movement by city):

1. For Model I, L has a range of 0.785 ± 0.019. Q gives a range of 0.909 ± 0.026. Model D correctly locates a proportion 0.913 ± 0.031, and Model U correctly locates a proportion 0.901 ± 0.047. That is, father-to-son mobility shows an increase in (quasi-) independence of about 10 percent for Models Q, D, and U, and of about 72 percent for Model I. (These percentages indicate the average increase in the level of L. The former would be much larger and the latter would be smaller if we normed the increase in L by the maximum *possible* increase.) When the main diagonal is dropped, about 90 per cent of the population is located correctly by supply and demand effects (in terms of the normed quantity L), more than when supply is defined by previous occupation.

2. Otherwise, the comments for grouping A apply except that Los Angeles does not (nor does any other city) show any difference between Models D and U. This interpretation is borne out by the pattern of L values for the Q, D, and U models, from which the stayer population has been removed.

In all cases the degree of independence increases substantially when the stayer (main diagonal and four near-diagonal) routes are

TABLE 12.

Intra-generational movement by city.

a. Philadelphia

Occupation in 1949

		I	II	III	IV	V
Occupation in 1940	I	186	16	8	6	6
	II	43	117	12	19	10
	III	16	6	180	37	9
	IV	21	21	42	211	26
	V	8	7	12	18	73

b. New Haven

Occupation in 1949

		I	II	III	IV	V
Occupation in 1940	I	225	15	13	14	1
	II	35	94	9	27	11
	III	32	3	184	19	8
	IV	30	25	55	208	36
	V	7	7	22	33	81

c. Chicago

Occupation in 1949

		I	II	III	IV	V
Occupation in 1940	I	202	19	18	12	2
	II	38	144	21	28	4
	III	27	6	205	20	6
	IV	32	15	63	184	24
	V	9	11	32	26	115

d. St. Paul

Occupation in 1949

		I	II	III	IV	V
Occupation in 1940	I	246	20	15	9	8
	II	43	127	13	17	5
	III	12	12	174	14	8
	IV	21	18	46	156	22
	V	8	21	12	29	83

e. San Francisco

Occupation in 1949

		I	II	III	IV	V
Occupation in 1940	I	225	36	13	12	10
	II	41	106	15	11	10
	III	25	5	142	4	9
	IV	24	19	41	91	31
	V	13	3	14	16	132

f. Los Angeles

Occupation in 1949

		I	II	III	IV	V
Occupation in 1940	I	242	30	11	7	4
	II	43	76	9	4	5
	III	29	8	117	16	1
	IV	26	13	40	69	12
	V	11	5	17	19	51

TABLE 13.

Inter-generational movement by city.

a. Philadelphia

Occupation of respondent

		I	II	III	IV	V
Occupation of father	I	115	25	59	52	13
	II	43	36	47	30	18
	III	32	11	121	64	29
	IV	42	13	98	95	51
	V	17	5	32	26	25

b. New Haven

Occupation of respondent

		I	II	III	IV	V
Occupation of father	I	163	20	89	42	34
	II	55	15	46	39	16
	III	49	8	106	60	56
	IV	45	12	86	97	52
	V	10	5	28	32	40

c. Chicago

Occupation of respondent

		I	II	III	IV	V
Occupation of father	I	135	31	75	36	30
	II	47	37	54	49	21
	III	43	16	143	79	50
	IV	37	13	78	78	47
	V	29	10	29	21	24

d. St. Paul

Occupation of respondent

		I	II	III	IV	V
	I	153	34	97	36	20
Occupation of father	II	60	25	64	36	23
	III	35	14	104	42	21
	IV	29	10	83	49	31
	V	11	9	36	25	37

e. San Francisco

Occupation of respondent

		I	II	III	IV	V
	I	174	27	72	16	30
Occupation of father	II	91	22	37	11	16
	III	50	13	74	22	26
	IV	18	5	31	25	36
	V	43	8	40	27	44

f. Los Angeles

Occupation of respondent

		I	II	III	IV	V
	I	190	39	71	23	16
Occupation of father	II	61	19	31	11	8
	III	50	10	57	34	17
	IV	32	5	34	18	17
	V	19	3	25	6	9

79

TABLE 14.

ϕ^2, e, Δ, and L for each of the "Six Cities" tables and models.

	Model			
	I	Q	D	U
ϕ^2 for each of the "Six Cities" Tables and Models				
Intra-generational movement by city				
Philadelphia	1.485	0.037	0.051	0.025
New Haven	1.311	0.132	0.088	0.090
Chicago	1.458	0.050	0.031	0.039
St. Paul	1.473	0.068	0.036	0.085
San Francisco	1.366	0.074	0.027	0.053
Los Angeles	1.141	0.062	0.141	0.009
Inter-generational movement by city				
Philadelphia	0.172	0.010	0.015	0.002
New Haven	0.153	0.020	0.021	0.013
Chicago	0.139	0.026	0.015	0.024
St. Paul	0.156	0.013	0.012	0.013
San Francisco	0.164	0.011	0.006	0.015
Los Angeles	0.112	0.008	0.004	0.003
e for each of the "Six Cities" Tables and Models				
Intra-generational movement by city				
Philadelphia	1.022	0.201	0.250	0.152
New Haven	1.311	0.132	0.088	0.090
Chicago	1.003	0.204	0.202	0.219
St. Paul	0.981	0.213	0.174	0.247
San Francisco	0.946	0.241	0.155	0.238
Los Angeles	0.952	0.286	0.374	0.093
Inter-generational movement by city				
Philadelphia	0.367	0.086	0.123	0.048
New Haven	0.329	0.170	0.141	0.169
Chicago	0.299	0.152	0.111	0.146
St. Paul	0.336	0.124	0.112	0.138
San Francisco	0.392	0.085	0.076	0.107
Los Angeles	0.373	0.067	0.071	0.070

TABLE 14 (Cont.)

	Model			
	I	Q	D	U

Δ for each of the "Six Cities" Tables and Models

Intra-generational
movement by city

Philadelphia	0.476	0.075	0.092	0.061
New Haven	0.444	0.147	0.106	0.114
Chicago	0.467	0.085	0.082	0.060
St. Paul	0.478	0.106	0.082	0.116
San Francisco	0.453	0.115	0.064	0.087
Los Angeles	0.411	0.079	0.126	0.034

Inter-generational
movement by city

Philadelphia	0.157	0.030	0.043	0.018
New Haven	0.154	0.053	0.058	0.033
Chicago	0.150	0.064	0.049	0.065
St. Paul	0.158	0.042	0.051	0.029
San Francisco	0.175	0.042	0.031	0.053
Los Angeles	0.150	0.037	0.025	0.024

L for each of the "Six Cities" Tables and Models

Intra-generational
movement by city

Philadelphia	0.467	0.861	0.802	0.851
New Haven	0.502	0.745	0.754	0.761
Chicago	0.486	0.831	0.825	0.885
St. Paul	0.452	0.884	0.857	0.764
San Francisco	0.502	0.803	0.870	0.828
Los Angeles	0.521	0.846	0.775	0.919

Inter-generational
movement by city

Philadelphia	0.793	0.934	0.907	0.948
New Haven	0.803	0.899	0.882	0.901
Chicago	0.800	0.883	0.895	0.854
St. Paul	0.786	0.914	0.904	0.933
San Francisco	0.766	0.909	0.936	0.874
Los Angeles	0.772	0.927	0.944	0.936

excluded, or held constant, but particularly for the older ages of intra-generational movement. Roughly between 80 per cent and 90 per cent of the cases are located correctly *beyond* the minimum which must be located correctly by the marginals. That is, given that we know a person has moved, there is only a 10 per cent to 20 per cent (standardized) chance that his movement has not been independent of his origin. We had anticipated in earlier chapters that by conditioning on the mover-stayer dichotomy we could approach independence. We had not anticipated, however, that the conditioned and unconditioned (quasi-independent and independent) models would both produce such high values of L and such small values of ϕ^2 and e.

There is a definite pattern to the departures from the I and Q models, shown in results not given here. The non-random effects which govern the location of a minority of the population operate according to the ordinality of the classes; that is, the model of (quasi-) independence repeatedly over-estimates the number making "long" moves and under-estimates the number making "short" moves, as anticipated in Chapter 1. Ascription, in some form, does play a role.

The 5 x 5 table does not reveal any consistent pattern of departures from the U and D models. Since these models consist of only three sub-diagonals, however, distance from the main diagonal is only crudely measurable.

6.3 Blau and Duncan 17-category tables

We now consider the Blau and Duncan (1967) study of occupational mobility in the United States, based on a 1962 sample of males age 25—64 in the civilian non-institutional population. Blau and Duncan (1967, pp. 496, 498) present two 17-category tables describing frequency of mobility routes from father's occupation to respondent's occupation in 1962, and from respondent's first occupation to occupation in 1962. (We shall exclude an eighteenth category for "no answer".) Observed sample frequencies were weighted up to the population total, so that statistical tests are not possible with the frequencies given by Blau and Duncan. The actual sample size was 20,700, however, so that cell proportions are unusually stable for a large mobility table.

In this section we report on results of application of quasi-independent models to the tables of inter- and intra-generational mobility. The seventeen categories are defined by the following list. There is a general ordinality in prestige of the categories, but ordinality is not maintained for all component categories of all pairs of occupational groups. That is, some titles in category 9 have more prestige than some titles in category 4, for example. The most heterogeneous category is probably that of the farmer, since it includes such a range in size and type of farm.

1. Professionals, Self-employed
2. Professionals, Salaried
3. Managers
4. Salesmen, Not Retail
5. Proprietors
6. Clerical
7. Salesmen, Retail
8. Craftsmen, Manufacturing
9. Craftsmen, Other
10. Craftsmen, Construction
11. Operatives, Manufacturing
12. Operatives, Other
13. Operatives, Service
14. Laborers, Manufacturing
15. Laborers, Other
16. Farmers
17. Farm laborers

Figure 3 gives the numbers of unblocked cells and degrees of freedom for the four basic models, I, Q, D, and U. These models are themselves not shown in a figure because they are defined basically as before. For Model I, no cells are blocked. For Model Q, we constrain to zero an 8 x 8 block in the upper left, an 8 x 8 block in the lower right, and cell (9, 9). As developed in Chapter 5, Model Q is the minimal blocking which includes the main diagonal, recognizes the ordinality of categories, and has most degrees of freedom (see Appendix 4). Models D and U hold out all cells except the upper and lower triangles, respectively. In addition, in order to have no rows or columns with a single unconstrained cell (or the appearance of an unconstrained cell, since in such a situation the marginals determine single cells) we block out cells (1, 2), (2, 1), (16, 17), and (17, 16).

a. Model I (no cells blocked)

    Number of free cells   = 289
    Number of degrees of freedom = 256

b. Model Q

    Number of free cells   = 160
    Number of degrees of freedom = 127

c. Models D and U

    Number of free cells   = 134
    Number of degrees of freedom = 105

Fig. 3. Description of the 17 x 17 models.

The cell frequencies are available in Blau and Duncan and will not be presented here. We shall refer to their inter- and intra-generational tables as F–S (father-to-son) and S–S (son-to-son), respectively.

It was not possible to compute Δ_{max} for most 17 x 17 blockings, so $L = 1 - \Delta/\Delta_{max}$ cannot be given. For large tables the algorithm of Appendix 6 appears inadequate in the identification of blocks of cells with separable degrees of freedom. This inadequacy should be capable of correction for later use. However, Δ_{max} will be close to unity for large tables, as the marginals impose less restriction on the range of interior patterns of frequencies. We simply report the value of the unadjusted Δ for the 17 x 17 and 15 x 15 tables.

Table 15 gives the values of ϕ^2, e, and Δ for the Blau-Duncan F–S and S–S tables. In the absence of the measure L, I prefer to rely most on ϕ^2, since in other sections it rank-correlates so highly with L. We observe this pattern in Table 15: (1) There is a sharp increase in quasi-independence in Models Q, D, and U as compared to Model I. (2) Models Q, D, and U show approximately the same levels of quasi-independence. (3) There is less quasi-independence in the S–S table than in the F–S table (in *intra*-than in *inter*-generational movement). However, most of this difference is in Model I; for the other three models, the F–S and S–S tables show more nearly equal levels of quasi-independence. (4) The values of Δ are in the range of values of Δ for the 9 x 9 international tables (see Chapter 7).

The average absolute value of the relative error (e) for the F–S table is also in the range of e for the 9 x 9 international inter-generational tables. We can use the 17 x 17 table to make a more detailed inquiry into the location of the errors as a function of distance from the main diagonal. For this purpose I prefer to use the S–S table since it shows a higher level of error and its pattern is slightly more pronounced. The pattern for the F–S table is similar, but will not be shown. The pattern for Model U is not shown because it shows the same structure as Model Q. Table 16 summarizes the errors by their distance from the main diagonal.

For Models I, Q, and D, the rank correlation (Spearman's R) of k with e'_k are 0.998, −0.147, and 0.044, respectively. The first of these correlations is statistically significantly different from zero at a very high level, but the second two are not different from zero. There is not a tendency for the Q and D (and U) models to overestimate the amount of distant movement and to under-

TABLE 15.

ϕ^2, e, and Δ for Blau-Duncan tables F–S (father-to-son) and S–S (son-to-son). Farm categories included.

Measure and Table		Model			
		I	Q	D	U
ϕ^2	F–S	0.374	0.057	0.082	0.055
	S–S	0.855	0.073	0.083	0.074
e	F–S	0.553	0.332	0.358	0.237
	S–S	0.782	0.481	0.548	0.260
Δ	F–S	0.207	0.094	0.100	0.089
	S–S	0.271	0.103	0.083	0.113

TABLE 16.

e (the average relative error) and e' (the average absolute value of the relative error) for the S–S table on Models I, Q, and D for fixed distance from main diagonal.

$k=\|i-j\|$	Model I		Model Q		Model D	
	e_k	e'_k	e_k	e'_k	e_k	e'_k
0	5.015	5.015	0.000	0.000	0.000	0.000
1	0.482	0.684	0.139	0.171	-0.019	0.150
2	0.070	0.431	0.054	0.327	-0.034	0.262
3	0.074	0.501	-0.103	0.295	0.236	0.471
4	-0.224	0.404	-0.173	0.231	-0.088	0.285
5	-0.271	0.382	-0.098	0.300	-0.009	0.262
6	-0.315	0.436	-0.055	0.196	-0.055	0.385
7	-0.341	0.378	-0.174	0.333	0.487	0.540
8	-0.462	0.462	0.066	0.263	0.067	0.344
9	-0.597	0.597	-0.169	0.310	-0.294	0.452
10	-0.630	0.630	-0.132	0.264	-0.251	0.452
11	-0.623	0.623	0.144	0.522	0.378	1.223
12	-0.683	0.683	-0.150	0.504	-0.639	0.656
13	-0.811	0.811	-0.364	0.407	-0.633	0.667
14	-0.718	0.718	1.631	1.871	3.123	3.123
15	-0.896	0.896	-0.046	0.673	-0.466	0.533
16	-0.715	0.715	8.060	8.072	10.729	10.729

estimate the amount of near movement, as there is for Model I. But for Models Q and D, the rank correlations of k with e_k are 0.806 and 0.841, respectively, both of which are statistically different from zero with high probability. That is, the errors become larger

85

in an *absolute* sense as we move from the main diagonal, even though they do not tend to become more positive or more negative. Models Q and D (and U) correct the best known shortcoming of Model I, viz., the monotonic pattern of error for longer moves. But they introduce (or exaggerate) a second type of error, viz., a monotonic increase in *variance* of error for longer moves. There is randomness in sign, but not in absolute value of error with increased distance.

Moves into cells (1, 17) and (17, 1) (k = 16) show very great levels of error. However, this occurs partly because the number of such moves is small, and the effect on e is small because only two cells are involved.

A more detailed analysis would consider all cells. We shall not examine the table of errors in detail because of the evidence of considerable randomness in errors. The non-randomness that does exist suggests the introduction of additional multiplicative factors as described by Goodman (1970).

6.4 Exclusion of the farm occupations

It was suggested earlier (in Chapter 5) that movement in and out of the farm category is less random, because of the importance of land, equipment, and farm experience to prospective farmers, and because of the limited access by farm sons to skills for other occupations (nevertheless, of course, there is a high volume of sons moving into non-farm jobs).

We, like other researchers, have ranked farm occupations at the low end of the prestige hierarchy. When these occupations are

a. <u>Model I</u> (no cells blocked)
   Number of free cells   = 225
   Number of degrees of freedom = 196

b. <u>Model Q</u>
   Number of free cells   = 126
   Number of degrees of freedom = 97

c. <u>Models D and U</u>
   Number of free cells   = 103
   Number of degrees of freedom = 78

Fig. 4. Description of the 15 × 15 models
(for non-farm U.S. tables).

removed, therefore, two effects which may improve the general level of quasi-independence are confounded. For one thing, farm occupations have a special character; for another, by dropping them we reduce the range of possible moves. If farm occupations had intermediate prestige, say, then the latter effect would not be present. I know of no easy way to separate these two confounded effects, but they both lead to an increase in the level of quasi-independence. Figure 4 describes the I, Q, D, and U Models for the 15 × 15 tables that are obtained when farm categories are dropped. Model Q blocks different specific cells than for the 17 × 17 table; the other blockings constrain the same cells. The Q Model could have been defined alternatively to be identical to the Q Model for the 17 × 17 table but with the last two categories deleted.

Table 17 is analogous to Table 15 in its presentation of ϕ^2, e, and Δ for the F−S (father-to-son) and S−S (son-to-son) non-farm U.S. tables. It is difficult to evaluate the difference between Tables 17 and 15, i.e., the effect of dropping the farm category. On the basis of previous work (Wiley, 1966) we are rather sure that most differences are statistically significant. We cannot test for significance in the Blau-Duncan tables, since we do not have actual cell frequencies. If we did have them, only a simple χ^2 test would be required.

The most interesting feature of the comparison is that the U model is less affected than the D model. We infer that movement *into* (downward movement) farms is less random than movement *out of* farms. That is, it is easier for farmers and farm laborers to

TABLE 17.

ϕ^2, e, and Δ for Blau-Duncan tables F−S (father-to-son) and S−S (son-to-son). *Farm categories excluded*

Measure and Table		Model			
		I	Q	D	U
ϕ^2	F−S	0.267	0.057	0.067	0.057
	S−S	0.704	0.066	0.064	0.078
e	F−S	0.473	0.255	0.265	0.230
	S−S	0.750	0.355	0.436	0.273
Δ	F−S	0.184	0.095	0.095	0.095
	S−S	0.257	0.097	0.075	0.117

obtain the skills necessary for non-farm occupations than it is for non-farm sons to obtain the skills, etc., for farm work.

Such an explanation may apply to inter-generational movement, but it is less likely to hold for the S—S table. On Model U, and only on this model, ϕ^2, e, and Δ all indicate *less* quasi-independence when farms are excluded. The inference is that persons who once held a farm occupation, but now do not, have moved more independently of their farm origin than do persons with non-farm origins. This result strengthens a "boundary" concept, whereby farm jobs are not necessarily at the bottom of an *opportunity* hierarchy, but that they form a distinct and separate class. Then movement from the farm class does not imply the range of distance between non-farm pairs of jobs that operate for someone initially in the non-farm structure. This boundary effect operates most strongly for persons with the most powerful farm backgrounds, i.e., those whose first job was on a farm. Apparently, when such a person *does* move into the non-farm range of jobs, his latter job will be even more independent of his (farm) origin than if it were his father who had held the farm origin (F—S movement). We do not wish to exaggerate the importance of this unexpected pattern in the data. Further investigation would (a) deal separately with farm and farm laborer groups, (b) subdivide the farm category into more homogeneous status groups, (c) experiment with different locations of farmers in the prestige hierarchy represented by our numbering system, (d) evaluate the confounding effect described earlier when highest or lowest strata are blocked out.

6.5 The effect of collapsing a table: Part I

We shall briefly compare the results of three different uses of the Blau-Duncan non-farm inter-generational mobility table (F—S, farm excluded). In Chapter 7 we shall use 5×5 and 9×9 collapses, and in Section 6.4 we used the basic 15×15 table. To what degree will the models be affected by the collapsing of a basic table? We recognize at the outset that only a partial answer is possible with a single basic table; a thorough answer would require (in part) examination of different size collapses of several basic tables.

Table 18 brings together results using Blau-Duncan data that were presented in Table 17 and that will appear in Chapter 7. It shows a marked increase in ϕ^2, e, and Δ as the number of cells is

TABLE 18.

ϕ^2, e, Δ, and L for different versions of the Blau-Duncan U.S. inter-generational (F–S) table for non-farm males.

Measure and size of table		Model			
		I	Q	D	U
ϕ^2	5 × 5	0.144	0.007	0.002	0.009
	9 × 9	0.192	0.027	0.028	0.028
	15 × 15	0.267	0.057	0.067	0.057
e	5 × 5	0.375	0.084	0.050	0.114
	9 × 9	0.376	0.186	0.196	0.189
	15 × 15	0.473	0.255	0.265	0.230
Δ	5 × 5	0.159	0.029	0.014	0.034
	9 × 9	0.168	0.059	0.056	0.062
	15 × 15	0.184	0.095	0.095	0.095
L	5 × 5	0.789	0.943	0.958	0.914
	9 × 9	0.783	0.907	0.900	0.906
	15 × 15	–	–	–	–

increased. It should be observed that for Model I, the number of cases is unchanged as the number of cells is increased; for Model Q, it is reduced, and for Models D and U it is increased. We observe that the proportional increase in ϕ^2, e, and Δ for finer subdivision is least for Model I. It is much greater for Models Q, D, and U, and is consistently greater for D than for U.

Disaggregation *necessarily* increases Δ; ϕ^2 and e are not forced to increase but in virtually any application they will do so. The informational measure $I(\theta)$ of Section 5.3, to which ϕ^2 is approximately proportional, can be corrected for disaggregation (see Theil and Finizza, 1971). I know of no such corrections for e and Δ.

There is general agreement over collapses and over measures in the adequacy of the models. That is, if $>$ indicates that one model is more appropriate (fits better) than another, then $D > Q > U > I$.

The main conclusion is that the size of a table has a great deal to do with the level of its evaluative measure. Whenever possible, comparisons should be made between tables with the same number of categories. One can imagine situations in which certain sizes of tables would be incompatible with the basic structure. For example, some categorical variables (e.g., "caste" in any strongly caste-based societies) may require exactly J_1 categories in one instance and exactly J_2 categories in another instance. For such a case the lack of comparability may completely obviate use of the models. However, a researcher should at least (a) collapse the larger table to the size of the smaller one, or (b) delete some categories from the larger table in order to minimize the simple effect of table size on level of fit.

6.6 The effect of collapsing a table: Part II

Given that a basic 17×17 table has been collapsed to a 9×9 table, say, how sensitive is the model to the grouping which led to the smaller table? This section responds to this aspect of the aggregation problem by comparing results for several ways of collapsing the 17×17 Blau-Duncan inter-generational (F–S, including farm) table for the U.S. Figure 5 describes the grouping in the six 9×9 collapses we shall consider.

Collapses 1–4 would probably not be used for any purpose other than the present one. The first three involve simple combina-

Collapse # 1		Collapse # 2		Collapse # 3	
I	1–9	I	1	I	1
II	10	II	2	II	2
III	11	III	3	III	3
IV	12	IV	4	IV	5
V	13	V	5–13	V	5
VI	14	VI	14	VI	6
VII	15	VII	15	VII	7
VIII	16	VIII	16	VIII	8
IX	17	IX	17	IX	9–17

Collapse # 4		Collapse # 5		Collapse # 6	
I	1–5	I	1–4	I	1–2
II	6	II	5–7	II	3–4
III	7	III	8	III	5
IV	8	IV	9–10	IV	6–7
V	9	V	11	V	8–10
VI	10	VI	12–13	VI	11–12
VII	11	VII	14–15	VII	13
VIII	12	VIII	16	VIII	14–15
IX	13–17	IX	17	IX	16–17

Fig. 5. Definitions of categories in collapsed tables. Roman numerals, our designations; arabic numerals, original designations.

tion of the first nine, the middle nine, and the last nine categories, respectively, into a single group. For each we place nearly half the population into a single group and keep the rest divided over eight groups. The result is a set of marginals which is far from uniform. Collapse 4 involves gathering the first five categories into a single group and the last five into a single group. The remaining seven categories are left separated. The departure from non-uniform marginals is not so severe for this collapse as for the previous three.

Collapse 5 is rather arbitrary and was created not with a view toward preserving "natural" groupings of categories, but with the objective of being intermediate to Collapses 1—4 and the substantive Collapse 6. Collapse 6 is identical to panel e of Table 19 and is derived from natural groupings of the Blau-Duncan categories. Collapse 5 (a) is a grouping that someone unfamiliar with occupational definitions could conceivably have gathered, (b) displaces a component occupation by no more than two (roman numeral) groups from Collapse 6, (c) is not drastically non-uniform in its marginals, as compared with Collapses 1—4. We are, therefore, particularly interested in the sensitivity of the results to Collapses 5 and 6.

The six panels of Table 19 give the results for each of these six collapses. We note the following patterns. For the four artificial collapses (1—4), Model Q is least appropriate, by far. That is, by including a large, heterogeneous category we reduce the level of quasi-independence markedly on Model Q, but not so much (if at all) on the other models. Evidently a large, heterogeneous category distorts origin and destination effects. This distortion is greatest for Collapses 1, 2, and 4, in which aggregation has occurred at the upper and/or lower strata. For these collapses, the large, compacted category does not appear in both the downward and upward triangles of the Q model, although it does for Collapse 2, when the large category is the "pivotal" category of Model Q. We should expect greatest distortion when the aggregated category is common to both upward and downward movers because of the link this pivotal category provides. But the distortion is least (among Collapses 1—4) for Collapse 2. We therefore conclude that

(a) Model Q is most sensitive to aggregation of the high and/or low categories, and less sensitive to aggregation of intermediate categories. Of all the models, Model Q is most sensitive to aggregation.

Major artificial Collapses (1—4) all *improve* the fit on Model I

TABLE 19.

Results for six collapses of the 17×17 Blau-Duncan F—S table into size 9×9.

	Model			
	I	Q	D	U
Measure: ϕ^2				
Collapse 1	0.232	0.787	0.037	0.018
Collapse 2	0.261	0.371	0.037	0.007
Collapse 3	0.202	0.804	0.032	0.034
Collapse 4	0.214	0.812	0.026	0.018
Collapse 5	0.302	0.030	0.029	0.025
Collapse 6	0.296	0.027	0.027	0.026
Measure: e				
Collapse 1	0.530	0.803	0.235	0.179
Collapse 2	0.925	1.009	0.525	0.229
Collapse 3	0.744	0.987	0.214	0.236
Collapse 4	0.319	0.723	0.164	0.142
Collapse 5	0.498	0.212	0.213	0.160
Collapse 6	0.461	0.203	0.223	0.170
Measure: Δ				
Collapse 1	0.170	0.342	0.060	0.046
Collapse 2	0.139	0.115	0.036	0.018
Collapse 3	0.158	0.270	0.059	0.061
Collapse 4	0.185	0.331	0.063	0.048
Collapse 5	0.192	0.070	0.054	0.064
Collapse 6	0.187	0.065	0.053	0.061
Measure: L				
Collapse 1	–	0.387	0.882	0.921
Collapse 2	0.735	0.528	0.849	0.946
Collapse 3	0.648	0.512	–	0.869
Collapse 4	0.775	0.498	0.917	0.926
Collapse 5	–	0.893	0.914	0.901
Collapse 6	0.763	0.902	0.913	0.900

for the measure ϕ^2, which weights squared errors inversely to their expectations (which will be large for aggregated cells). This result is not supported by e, Δ, and L. We conclude that

(*b*) Model I, the usual model of independence, is not particularly sensitive to the form of the collapse, with respect to direction of variation.

Models D and U, the models of downward and upward movement, are variously higher and lower on each measure for the first four collapses relative to the last two. There is substantial variation (e.g., measure e on Model D ranges from 0.164 to 0.525) but it does not seem to be consistent with respect to direction of movement, measure, or collapse. That is,

(c) The models for upward and downward movement are affected more like Model I than Model Q, in that "extreme" collapses may show either more or less quasi-independence than "substantive" or "uniform" collapses.

Finally, comparison of Collapses 5 and 6, introduced earlier as relatively uniform and not widely different, show very close correspondence, differing by no more than about 5 per cent on measures ϕ^2, e, Δ, and L. These two collapses differ in definition by about the maximum amount that we would expect from two different researchers who independently collapsed the U.S. table from size 17 x 17 to size 9 x 9. But they agree nearly perfectly in results, so we can conclude that

(d) Relative to international variation in level of quasi-independence (see Chapter 7), the effect introduced by alternative but similar collapses of data is negligible.

It is advised that when possible, in order to get a better grasp of the effect of category definitions, comparative work employ several "reasonable" collapses, i.e., collapses motivated by the joint criteria of the formal definitions of occupations and of a near-uniform marginal distribution. Interpretation could then be more confidently based on the *range* of results, which, on the basis of this section, I believe would be narrow.

CHAPTER 7

Quasi-independence applied to international mobility tables

7.1 Nine 3 × 3 tables

In this chapter we extend the various versions of quasi-independence to three groups of inter-generational mobility tables from different countries. To improve comparability, each group is homogeneous with respect to number and, to an extent, with respect to definitions of categories.

The objective is, as in Chapter 6, to describe the level and variability in the model's fit, and to arrange tables within groups according to their degree of ascription in inter-class movement.

We begin with a basic set of nine 3 × 3 tables collected in *Social Mobility in Industrial Society*, by S.M. Lipset and R. Bendix (1964). (Sources of data are described therein.) All tables are organized according to non-manual, manual, and farm occupational groupings. All are based on post-war studies, ranging generally from the middle 1940's to middle 1950's. All are based on national samples, not simply urban samples, in contrast to the tables from the U.S. Six Cities Study.

The principal conclusion of Lipset and Bendix drawn from these tables was that, in gross terms, there is little variation in post-war, industrial (including Japan) mobility patterns. This conclusion was not derived from statistical tests, but from the authors' notion of how much variation would be substantively significant. Their principal interest, in this regard, was in proportions of persons moving from non-manual to manual occupations, etc.

Through quasi-independent models we are able to reduce the data of these tables to individual measures of departure from a completely open structure — over the total population, or over a

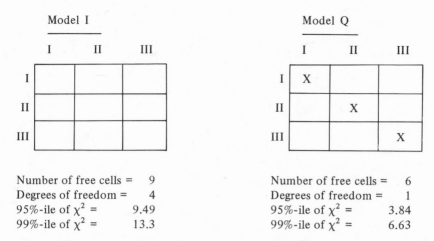

Model I				Model Q		
	I	II	III		I	II	III
I				I	X		
II				II		X	
III				III			X

Number of free cells = 9   Number of free cells = 6
Degrees of freedom = 4   Degrees of freedom = 1
95%-ile of χ^2 = 9.49   95%-ile of χ^2 = 3.84
99%-ile of χ^2 = 13.3   99%-ile of χ^2 = 6.63

Fig. 6. The 3 × 3 models. X indicates a constrained cell.

sub-population, such as that of the movers only. Our goals are the same as those of the early part of *Social Mobility in Industrial Society*, but we make more complete use of the data with which Lipset and Bendix work.

Figure 6 illustrates the two basic models. Model I has the full four degrees of freedom of a 3 × 3 table, with no constrained cells. Model Q holds out the sub-population of stayers on the main diagonal, with only one degree of freedom left. It is, we believe, the most plausible quasi-independent model for a 3 × 3 table, because of the clarity of the mover-stayer dichotomy. It is not possible to construct a model for upward or downward movers alone and retain any degrees of freedom.

Table 20 reports, in nine panels, the basic data and measures for the nine tables. Rows indicate occupation of father, columns that of the respondent. There are three tables for Germany and two for the United States, so that only six countries are represented. However, we wish to delay recognition of the inclusion of multiple tables for Germany and the United States, and simply to regard these tables as nine different collections of data.

We have computed Spearman's rank correlation, R, for the correspondences among ϕ^2, e, and L. There is almost perfect agreement in order for Model Q. For Model I, agreement is highest between the rankings by ϕ^2 and L, with R = −0.850.

Table 21 also reports, in its upper right quadrant, the similarity between the Model I and Model Q rankings for each of the measures. The higher these rank correlations, the nearer the order

TABLE 20.

Data and results for nine international 3×3 tables. Rows represent father's occupational group; columns represent respondent's occupational group. Categories I, II, and III are non-manual, manual, and farm, respectively.

a. Germany 1

	I	II	III
I	336	220	23
II	110	276	20
III	23	34	66

	Model I	*Model Q*
N	1108	430
χ^2	399.16	0.15
ϕ^2	0.360	0.0003
e	0.876	0.027
Δ	0.205	0.006
Δ_{max}	0.643	0.160
L	0.682	0.961

b. Germany 2

	I	II	III
I	185	46	5
II	63	126	21
III	17	26	96

	Model I	*Model Q*
N	585	178
χ^2	374.18	1.28
ϕ^2	0.640	0.007
e	0.797	0.110
Δ	0.342	0.033
Δ_{max}	0.740	0.287
L	0.538	0.885

Table 20 (Cont.)

c. *Germany 3*

	I	II	III
I	186	74	5
II	77	209	12
III	32	39	88

	Model I	*Model Q*
N	722	239
χ^2	397.30	1.13
ϕ^2	0.550	0.005
e	0.821	0.101
Δ	0.303	0.023
Δ_{max}	0.726	0.151
L	0.583	0.846

d. *United States 1*

	I	II	III
I	226	80	13
II	150	263	17
III	92	158	154

	Model I	*Model Q*
N	1153	510
χ^2	355.96	4.90
ϕ^2	0.309	0.010
e	0.571	0.167
Δ	0.227	0.029
Δ_{max}	0.619	0.100
L	0.633	0.712

Table 20 (Cont.)

e. United States 2

	I	II	III
I	117	61	2
II	90	195	6
III	78	148	97

	Model I	*Model Q*
N	794	385
χ^2	200.00	0.01
ϕ^2	0.252	0.00002
e	0.562	0.011
Δ	0.193	0.0008
Δ_{max}	0.613	0.047
L	0.685	0.984

f. France

	I	II	III
I	809	200	100
II	219	343	63
III	206	167	916

	Model I	*Model Q*
N	3023	955
χ^2	1605.30	2.55
ϕ^2	0.531	0.003
e	0.668	0.056
Δ	0.344	0.023
Δ_{max}	0.794	0.314
L	0.580	0.925

Table 20 (Cont.)

g. *Japan*

	I	II	III
I	853	243	58
II	247	441	60
III	409	322	731

	Model I	*Model Q*
N	3364	1339
χ^2	1235.02	1.39
ϕ^2	0.367	0.001
e	0.587	0.043
Δ	0.272	0.012
Δ_{max}	0.757	0.134
L	0.641	0.910

h. *Sweden*

	I	II	III
I	150	47	6
II	105	231	25
III	71	129	107

	Model I	*Model Q*
N	871	383
χ^2	253.65	0.003
ϕ^2	0.291	0.000007
e	0.570	0.004
Δ	0.224	0.0008
Δ_{max}	0.642	0.196
L	0.652	0.996

Table 20 (Cont.)

i. Switzerland

	I	II	III
I	489	76	17
II	105	127	7
III	82	58	163

	Model I	*Model Q*
N	1124	345
χ^2	585.20	3.03
ϕ^2	0.521	0.009
e	0.778	0.137
Δ	0.287	0.032
Δ_{max}	0.632	0.148
L	0.545	0.782

TABLE 21.

Rank correlations (Spearman's R) between measures for the international 3×3 tables.

		Model I		*Model Q*		
		e	L	ϕ^2	e	L
Model I	ϕ^2	0.717*	− 0.850**	0.533		
	e		− 0.417		0.317	
	L					0.650*
Model Q	ϕ^2				1.000**	− 0.967**
	e					− 0.975**

*Significant at 0.05 level.
**Significant at 0.01 level.

of fit on the two models. The R values of 0.533, 0.317, and 0.650 indicate that there is only partial agreement, so that macro-level variables which determine the openness of the full pattern (Model I) differ (if only in relative impact) from those which determine the openness of the mover pattern alone (Model Q). A table can do well on one model but not on the other, although there is evidence for a small ("true") positive rank correlation. It may be, for example, that for one model, dispersal of wealth is more important than dispersal of education, whereas the reverse holds for the other model.

Table 22 illustrates how the low rank correlations between the two models may arise. P_m is the proportion of movers in the full 3×3 table. For Model I, this proportion correlates highly with the measures of fit. Thus, the higher the proportion of movers (i.e., the lower the proportion of persons on the main diagonal), the better Model I does. This relation is, of course, the motivation for holding out the main diagonal, which is the main source of departure from independence in Model I. Those factors which support a high proportion of stayers will also prevent Model I from accurately describing the mobility pattern. Note that the off-diagonal proportion P_m is in one sense *not* the proportion of movers. By the basic mover-stayer concept, some "movers" will be located on the main diagonal just by random movement, and not by actual inheritance. Goodman's "new index" of inheritance (1969b) would be preferable to P_m in this sense (the two should be inversely related).

Table 22 shows correlations among P_m and ϕ^2, e, and L for Model Q which are in the expected direction but are not signifi-

TABLE 22.

Rank correlations (Spearman's R) between P_m and measures for the international 3×3 tables

	Model I	Model Q
ϕ^2	− 0.900**	− 0.450
e	− 0.717*	− 0.450
L	0.850**	0.350

*Significant at 0.05 level.
**Significant at 0.01 level.

cantly different from zero. Factors *other* than those which promote a high proportion of stayers, not now specified, evidently limit the accuracy of Model Q.

Adequacy of models I and Q

We now return to Table 15, paying particular attention to L, the standardized proportion accurately placed by the model of (quasi-) independence, since it is the most easily interpretable measure.

For Model I, the range of L is centered at 0.612 and has a width of two times 0.074. We shall represent the range as 0.612 ± 0.074. That is, allowing for the marginal constraints, which limit the location of the interior frequencies to certain patterns, independence accounts for 61.2 per cent ± 7.4 per cent of the placement. Only about 39 per cent of the cases in each table indicate ascription. A range of 14.8 per cent for nine tables is so small that we agree at this point with Lipset and Bendix: there is little variation in gross pattern of movement. The range in Δ is *statistically* significant, but we do not believe it is substantively significant, partly because of the discrepancies between L, e, and ϕ^2 (see Figure 7).* The variation that does exist is mainly a manifestation of the variation in P_m.

For Model Q, L takes on values 0.853 ± 0.141. That is, when limited to the sub-population of movers, we correctly locate about 24 per cent additional cases, a relative gain over the full model of about 40 per cent. Clearly, again, ascription affects the main diagonal far more than the rest of the table.

	Order by L	Order by e	Order by ϕ^2
1	United States 2	United States 2	United States 2
2	Germany 1	Sweden	Sweden
3	Sweden	United States 1	United States 1
4	Japan	Japan	Germany 1
5	United States 1	France	Japan
6	Germany 3	Switzerland	Switzerland
7	France	Germany 2	France
8	Switzerland	Germany 3	Germany 3
9	Germany 2	Germany 1	Germany 2

Fig. 7. Order of the 3 × 3 tables on Model I by L, e, and ϕ^2, from best fit to worst fit.

* See footnote on p. 74.

The range in L is nearly doubled, to more than 28 per cent. Because of this range, and because of the very high inter-correlations of measures for Model Q (see the lower right quadrant of Table 21), we might infer that for Model Q, there is variation over the nine tables which is both statistically and substantively significant. We do *not* infer this, however, for the following reasons:

(1) The wider range in L is due mainly to the very small values of Δ_{max} for Model Q. The range in Δ itself is small.

(2) As Figure 8 shows, multiple tables for the same country (viz., United States 1 and 2) are widely separated. Readings of the same structure at nearly identical time points should not differ substantively.

(3) The high inter-correlations of the measures result mainly from the presence of only one degree of freedom. Despite the measures' different derivations, these formulae can be simplified to quite similar forms for the case of a single degree of freedom. Therefore, rather than three independent measures, we really have only one measure, stated three ways.

Less critical evidence that there is no variation of any significance is the apparent lack of relation of the ordering in Figure 8 to any other structural variations, such as the proportion mobile, the proportion with farm origin or destination, etc. There is also no relation to *changes* in the distribution over occupations. That L (or Δ), e, and ϕ^2 do not correlate with other characteristics is additional evidence that variation in these measures is random over the nine tables. We consider this finding to be a significant support of Lipset and Bendix (despite our restriction here, with them, to 3 x 3 tables).

	Order by L	Order by ϕ^2 and e
1	Sweden	Sweden
2	United States 2	United States 2
3	Germany 1	Germany 1
4	France	Japan
5	Japan	France
6	Germany 2	Germany 3
7	Germany 3	Germany 2
8	Switzerland	Switzerland
9	United States 1	United States 1

Fig. 8. Order of the 3 x 3 tables on Model Q by L and by ϕ^2 and e, from best fit to worst fit.

Finally, one might consider inquiring into the major source of relative error in Model Q. The errors are uniformly largest in cells of movement into farm occupation. Relative errors for these two routes have an average absolute relative error which is from two to twenty-two times the average absolute relative error for the other four routes of Model Q. However, there are two related reasons why this observation does not lead anywhere. First, since Model Q has only one degree of freedom, all six cells of movement have the same absolute error *in frequency*. This will appear as a large *relative* error in cells with small frequencies; cells of movement onto farms uniformly have the smallest frequencies, both expected and observed. Second, and closely related to the previous point, relative errors in the two cells of movement onto farms are highly rank-correlated with errors in the other cells, despite the larger values of the errors. Consequently, the pattern of errors cannot be of much use in the case of one degree of freedom.

7.2 Seven 5 × 5 tables

In this section we continue our inquiry into the variability of international mobility patterns, as indicated by their approach to (quasi-) independence. The findings of this section will be independent of those in the preceding section, since the seven tables used are based on samples completely independent of those which generated the 3 × 3 tables. They represent a completely different set of countries, except that the United States and Japan are included in both sets (with different samples).

Six of the tables were taken from an appendix to a lengthy paper by S.M. Miller (1960) which contains many useful, more substantively-oriented inferences about comparative social mobility. Miller's appendix listed twenty tables, but most of these were dropped for the following reasons: (a) I selected only tables with five or more non-farm categories, and (b) I excluded a few tables which satisfied (a) but used such narrow definitions of occupations that several cells had zero or near-zero frequencies. Five categories were used as a compromise between (a) the goal of using a table substantially larger than 3 × 3 to evaluate the models, and (b) the goal of using as many tables as possible from Miller's collection. Moreover, 5 × 5 tables were employed in Sections 6.1–6.2. We have seen in Section 6.5 that most kinds of comparisons are best made between tables of the same size, so many of the tables from Miller were collapsed from larger tables.

Figure 9 lists the sources given by Miller and the definitions of categories. The table from the U.S. is due to Blau and Duncan (1967, p. 496) and was obtained in 1962 in a Current Population Survey. The frequencies given are inflated from the sample to the total population. The actual sample frequencies are not given by Blau and Duncan because of the stratified nature of the sample. The total sample size, however, was 20,700, so large that the given table is highly stable, in terms of proportions. The remaining tables are slightly earlier; all come from the 1950's.

There is far from perfect comparability of occupational groups between tables, arising from two sources. First, some authors have specifically ranked by prestige (e.g., Svalastoga, 1959) and others by more immediate attributes of an occupation, such as a manual-non-manual distinction. As several persons have observed, however (e.g., Treiman, 1968), there is general international consensus about the prestige of occupations, and we expect that both types of rankings will agree closely. We also observe (in results not shown here) through departures from the model of independence (Model I) that there is an ordinality in the categories for each country, corresponding to a monotonic variation from high prestige (Category I) to low prestige (Category V).

The second difficulty in comparability is in a general upgrading or downgrading of categories in some tables relative to other tables. For example, semi-skilled manual labor is ranked higher in Poona, India, than in the United States. For some purposes, a

FIGURE 9.

a. Brazil

Source: B. Hutchinson (1958, p. 116)

I	1,2	Professional and high administrative; managerial and executive
II	3	Inspectional, supervisory, other non-manual, high
III	4	Inspectional, supervisory, other non-manual, low
IV	5	Skilled manual
V	6	Semi-skilled and unskilled manual

b. Denmark

Source: Svalastoga (1959, p. 331)

I	2,3,4	Upper and upper middle
II	5	Middle middle
III	6	Lower middle
IV	7	Upper lower
V	8,9	Lower lower

Fig. 9 (Cont.)

c. Great Britain

Source: Glass (1954, ch. 1)

I	1,2	Professional and high administrative, managerial and executive
II	3,4	Inspectional, supervisory, other non-manual
III	5a,6	Routine non-manual, skilled manual
IV	6	Semi-skilled manual
V	7	Unskilled manual

d. Japan

Source: S. Nishira (1957, p. 187)

I	1,2	Professional and administrative
II	3,4	Clerical, commercial
III	5	Skilled
IV	6	Semi-skilled
V	7	Unskilled

e. Poona (Source: Sovani and Pradhan, 1955, p. 123)

I	1,4	Owners of factories; higher and intermediate professional, business and administrative, medium merchants
II	5,6	Clerical, supervisory, highly skilled
III	7	Small business
IV	8,9	Lower professional and administrative, skilled manual
V	10	Unskilled manual

f. Puerto Rico

Source: M. M. Tumin and A. S. Feldman (1961, p. 372)

I	1,2	Professional and semi-professional
II	3,4	Owners of business, managers and white-collar sales
III	6,7	Clerks and office workers, skilled labor
IV	8	Semi-skilled labor
V	9,10	Service workers, unskilled labor

g. United States

Source: Blau and Duncan (1967, p. 496)

I	1,4	Professionals, managers, officials, proprietors
II	5,7	Sales, clerical
III	8,10	Craftsmen
IV	11,13	Operatives, service workers
V	14,15	Laborers

Fig. 9. Sources of data for international 5 × 5 tables and definitions of categories. (Roman numerals: our designation; arabic numbers: designation in source.)

106

precise correspondence among all categories of the same rank would be essential. For our purposes, it is important that there be few cells with very small frequencies. Thus we have tried to compromise between (a) the goal of perfect comparability and (b) the goal of statistically stable cell frequencies. As we saw in Section 6.5, alternative collapses of data have small effect on our summary measures.

The basic blockings or models are those illustrated in Figure 2 (see discussion in Section 6.2). The original tables are given in the seven panels of Table 23, and the value of ϕ^2, e, Δ and L are shown in Table 24.

Table 25 evaluates the correspondence among the measures within and between models I and Q. As with the 3 x 3 tables, we observe highly significant agreement, in rank correlation, between ϕ^2 and L within model I and within model Q. Other within-model rank correlations are in the direction of agreement, but are not statistically significant. Because ϕ^2 and L agree so closely, and rank correlations involving e are nearer zero, we shall restrict attention to the rankings on ϕ^2 and L. Moreover, since L is more interpretable, we shall, as before, give priority to the ranking on that measure.

Table 25 also shows small, but non-significant, correspondences *between* models I and Q. (See the upper right quadrant of Table 25.) As before, we conclude that there is only minor overlap between the sources of variation in fit to the two models.

TABLE 23.

Data and results for seven international 5 x 5 tables.

a. Brazil

Occupation of respondent

		I	II	III	IV	V
	I	84	26	6	2	0
	II	29	68	21	16	1
Occupation of father III	36	39	74	61	7
	IV	21	26	45	132	24
	V	10	29	41	142	116

Table 23 (Cont.)

b. *Denmark*

Occupation of respondent

		I	II	III	IV	V
Occupation of father	I	18	17	16	4	2
	II	24	105	109	59	21
	III	23	84	289	217	95
	IV	8	49	175	348	198
	V	6	8	69	201	246

c. *Great Britain*

Occupation of respondent

		I	II	III	IV	V
Occupation of father	I	297	92	172	37	26
	II	89	110	223	64	32
	III	164	185	714	258	189
	IV	25	40	179	143	71
	V	17	32	141	91	106

d. *Japan*

Occupation of respondent

		I	II	III	IV	V
Occupation of father	I	80	72	19	13	24
	II	44	155	26	21	45
	III	13	35	72	20	19
	IV	5	17	18	19	16
	V	77	177	90	67	722

e. Poona

Occupation of respondent

		I	II	III	IV	V
Occupation of father	I	344	168	27	47	27
	II	57	278	16	39	25
	III	73	70	151	49	34
	IV	89	244	51	554	148
	V	170	309	128	532	865

f. Puerto Rico

Occupation of respondent

		I	II	III	IV	V
Occupation of father	I	45	23	28	13	13
	II	32	47	47	20	54
	III	25	24	86	29	57
	IV	4	3	26	26	21
	V	15	18	35	37	68

g. United States

Occupation of respondent

		I	II	III	IV	V
Occupation of father	I	3184	906	698	660	108
	II	1203	490	357	362	63
	III	1851	784	1843	1421	302
	IV	1647	825	1591	2189	497
	V	307	257	498	783	313

TABLE 24.

ϕ^2, e, Δ, and L for the seven international 5×5 tables.

	Model			
	I	Q	D	U

ϕ^2 *for the International 5×5 Tables*

Brazil	0.622	0.021	0.013	0.022
Denmark	0.315	0.011	0.005	0.016
Great Britain	0.223	0.044	0.003	0.004
Japan	0.410	0.019	0.025	0.016
Poona	0.559	0.029	0.011	0.032
Puerto Rico	0.172	0.035	0.026	0.049
United States	0.144	0.007	0.002	0.009

e for the International 5×5 Tables

Brazil	0.679	0.214	0.279	0.135
Denmark	0.903	0.178	0.134	0.199
Great Britain	0.427	0.088	0.070	0.094
Japan	0.679	0.159	0.144	0.178
Poona	0.719	0.147	0.104	0.199
Puerto Rico	0.384	0.196	0.157	0.236
United States	0.375	0.084	0.050	0.114

Δ *for the International 5×5 Tables*

Brazil	0.287	0.046	0.033	0.054
Denmark	0.194	0.028	0.020	0.036
Great Britain	0.150	0.023	0.021	0.023
Japan	0.254	0.043	0.067	0.034
Poona	0.259	0.064	0.029	0.071
Puerto Rico	0.157	0.071	0.061	0.086
United States	0.159	0.029	0.014	0.034

L for the International 5×5 Tables

Brazil	0.610	0.908	0.819	0.901
Denmark	0.728	0.909	0.928	0.889
Great Britain	0.786	0.929	0.936	0.922
Japan	0.623	0.900	0.862	0.896
Poona	0.662	0.890	0.941	0.865
Puerto Rico	0.792	0.874	0.858	0.828
United States	0.789	0.943	0.958	0.914

TABLE 25.

Rank correlations (Spearman's R) between measures for the international 5 × 5 tables

		Model I		Model Q		
		e	L	ϕ^2	e	L
Model I	ϕ^2	0.661	− 0.929**	0.357		
	e		− 0.500		0.286	
	L					0.000
Model Q	ϕ^2				0.643	− 0.946**
	e					− 0.589

**Significant at 0.01 level.

Before looking further at the actual rankings on models, I, Q, D, and U, we can respond to one of our major objectives, a comparison of levels and variations of fit within the U.S. and outside of the U.S. For this purpose, Table 25 gives A) the midpoint of the range in L, and B) the semi-range of L for (1) the six intergenerational tables from the Six Cities Study described in Chapter 6 (representing each of the six cities), (2) the U.S. table of this chapter, and (3) the six non-U.S. tables of this section. All of these are 5 × 5 tables.

We offer the following qualifications to any comparison of columns one and two of Table 26. First, the U.S. table is based on a date of respondent's occupation which is about thirteen years, or half a generation, later than the date of the Six Cities tables. Second, there are slight differences in definitions of categories, although all are derived from U.S. Census definitions. Third, we used data from the Six Cities Study pertaining to white males only, to reduce heterogeneity, but the U.S. table refers to all males. Fourth, there are slight differences in the range of ages used. Fifth, and most important, the Six Cities data refer only to a non-randomly selected group of large urban places (with the exception of New Haven, which is not large), but the U.S. table is a randomly drawn representation of all non-farm males age 25−64 in the U.S.

In comparing columns one and three of Table 26 we must also consider that the six *non*-U.S. tables were not randomly selected, but were subject to availability and the restrictions mentioned

111

TABLE 26.

Comparison of variation and level of L for the models, using the Six Cities of the U.S. (Chapter 6), the whole U.S. (Blau-Duncan), and six non-U.S. tables. All are male, non-farm, inter-generational 5 × 5 tables. A denotes midpoint of range, B denotes semi-range.

		Six Cities Tables	U. S. Table	Six Non- U. S. Tables
Model I	A	0.785	0.789	0.701
	B	0.019		0.091
Model Q	A	0.909	0.943	0.902
	B	0.026		0.028
Model D	A	0.913	0.958	0.878
	B	0.031		0.059
Model U	A	0.901	0.914	0.875
	B	0.047		0.047

earlier. They do represent a wide range of political, economic, and social situations, but we could, needless to say, have extended the range further toward pre-industrialized societies, if data were available. Also, the average date of the six non-U.S. tables is about halfway between the dates of the U.S. Blau-Duncan table and the Six Cities tables.

Yet several factors favor comparability among the thirteen tables represented by Table 26. All are intra-generational, for non-farm males. All are collapsed into five categories. All are based on large samples. The numerical ranges in columns one and three refer to six tables each.

The principal patterns of Table 26 are these:

(1) For each model, the midpoint value of L is lowest for the six non-U.S. tables, intermediate for the Six Cities tables, and highest for the Blau-Duncan U.S. table.

(2) The midpoint value of L for the Six Cities tables consistently falls within the range of the six non-U.S. tables; the reverse is true or nearly true for the Q, D, and U models, but not for model I.

(3) For any given model, the greatest variation in the values of A is for model I. Here the U.S. table has a gain in level of L of 13 per cent over the midpoint value of L for the six non-U.S. tables. For the other models, in which we restrict ourselves to mobile sub-populations, the variability is smaller. On the basis of (2) and

112

(3), we infer that most international variation in pattern is due to the somewhat higher levels of inheritance (lower values of P_m) in the non-U.S. tables. The patterns in the mobile cells show less variability, in terms of departures from quasi-independence.

(4) L is uniformly higher, although only by small amounts, for the Blau-Duncan table than for the midpoint of the Six Cities tables. We do not wish to exaggerate the differences, but two opposing sources for some differences should be noted. On the one hand we could expect *higher* values of L for the Blau-Duncan data than for the Six Cities data because the Blau-Duncan study is more recent. We anticipate that father's occupation is a less important determinant over time, as the processes of industrialization, universal education, etc., are extended throughout the U.S. population.

On the other hand, we would expect *lower* values of L for the Blau-Duncan table because it has a different sampling universe — namely, the whole U.S. population (male, age 25–64, and, for us, non-farm). Achievement has been found to count for more, relative to ascription, in populations that are urban. The simple proportion of movement, P_m, is greater in large cities than in small cities, because of the greater range of occupations in large cities. Persons in large cities are more likely to have experienced geographical mobility than are persons in small cities, and occupational and geographical mobility are highly associated. Universalistic employment criteria are more common relative to particularistic criteria in large cities than in small cities. Education and technical skills are less dependent on father's status and occupation in large cities than in small cities.

Thus, if a sample such as the CPS sample of Blau and Duncan had been taken in 1949, we would expect it to give lower values of L than the Six Cities Study. If the Six Cities Study had been repeated in 1962, we would have expected higher values of L than in the original study.

(5) Finally, we observe from Table 28 that variability in the Six Cities does not exceed that of the six non-U.S. tables for any model, and except for model I, the ranges are comparable.

We now return to the actual ranking of the 5 × 5 tables on models I, Q, D, and U. Figure 10 lists the seven tables by their rankings on L and ϕ^2 for model I, the full model of independence. As in previous sets of tables, the rank on either ϕ^2 or L is very closely related to the rank of P_m, the proportion lying off the main diagonal. The difference between the best and worst fits is

	Order by L	Order by ϕ^2
1	Puerto Rico	United States
2	United States	Puerto Rico
3	Great Britain	Great Britain
4	Denmark	Denmark
5	Poona	Japan
6	Japan	Poona
7	Brazil	Brazil

Fig. 10. Order of the 5×5 tables on Model I using the measures L and ϕ^2, from best to worst fit.

statistically significant, but is small. Over all seven tables, L takes on the range 0.701 ± 0.091 for this model. Most differences *within* the ordering are not statistically significant; for example, Puerto Rico may quite possibly be third or lower in "true" rank, rather than first or second.

On the basis of these tables, we can infer that the international range in the standardized proportion correctly placed by the full inter-generational model is roughly between 0.60 and 0.80 for five categories of non-farm occupations. Both the high level of independence and the relatively narrow range are striking.

The order by L and ϕ^2 on model Q is given in Figure 11. The range represented in L is 0.909 ± 0.035, an increase of 30 per cent relative to the midpoint of the range for model I, and a reduction of 62 per cent in the semi-range. That is, of all persons in one of the sixteen mobile routes of model Q, an adjusted (normed) proportion of about 90 per cent, with *very* little variation over countries, has an occupation independent of father's occupation. There are few differences in Figure 11 that are statistically significant. There is clearly a general correspondence in rank with level of industrialization or modernity, not measured, despite the narrow range.

For model D, L takes on the range 0.889 ± 0.070. For model U, L takes on the range 0.875 ± 0.047. With earlier tables, we observed that model Q tended to be intermediate to Models U and D. For the present set of tables, using L, one could conclude that Q is superior to U and D. Note that the mid-point value of L for Model Q is within the range of L on both Models U and D.

Our overall conclusion is that specification of whether movement was upward or downward increases only slightly the level of independence. The increase in range relative to the Q model is probably a reflection of the increase in statistical

114

		Order by L	Order by ϕ^2
1		United States	Great Britain
2		Great Britain	United States
3	tied	Brazil	Denmark
4		Denmark	Japan
5		Japan	Brazil
6		Poona	Poona
7		Puerto Rico	Puerto Rico

Fig. 11. Order of the 5×5 tables on Model Q using the measures L and ϕ^2, from best to worst fit.

variation as the effective sample size is reduced (by about one-half relative to the Q model).

7.3 Five 9 × 9 tables

We conclude this chapter with a brief review of five intergenerational 9 x 9 tables. Few international tables are available which have more than nine categories and stable (large) frequencies. The tables used here represent a range of industrialization or modernization. Poona (India) and Puerto Rico are two relatively non-industrial situations. Aarhus (Denmark) represents an intermediate situation, and the United States represents a modern, industrialized society. The U.S. table is used twice, once with and once without the farm laborer category. The table from Puerto Rico also includes farm laborers. The sources of the tables and the definitions of categories are given in Figure 12. The categories in the table for Aarhus are rearranged from the original ordering, in order to achieve closer correspondence with the other tables' definitions.

FIGURE 12.

a. Aarhus, Denmark

Source: Theodor Geiger (1951)

I	4,9,6	Free professionals, ministers, teachers, technicians
II	5,7	Higher officials, managers
III	2,3	Proprietors, self-employed artisans
IV	10	Sales
V	11	Clerical
VI	13	Skilled workers
VII	8,15	Traffic personnel, apprentices
VIII	12	Residual salaried
IX	14	Unskilled workers

b. Poona, India
Source: Sovani and Pradhan (1955, p. 25)

I	1,2	Owners of factories, higher professional, business, administrative
II	3	Medium merchants
III	4	Intermediate professional, business and administrative
IV	5	Clerks and shop assistants
V	6	Highly skilled and supervisory
VI	7	Small business
VII	8	Lower professional, administrative
VIII	9	Skilled manual workers
IX	10	Unskilled manual workers

c. Puerto Rico (including farm)
Source: Tumin and Feldman (1961, p. 130)

I	1	Professional
II	2	Semi-professional
III	3,4	Owners of business, managers and white-collar sales
IV	6	Clerks and office workers
V	7	Skilled labor
VI	8	Semi-skilled labor
VII	9	Service workers
VIII	10	Unskilled labor
IX	11	Agricultural day labor

d. United States
Source: Blau and Duncan (1967, p. 496)

I	1,2	Professionals
II	3,4	Managers and salesmen, not retail
III	5	Proprietors
IV	6	Clerical
V	7	Salesmen, retail
VI	8,9 & 10	Craftsmen
VII	11,12	Operatives
VIII	13	Service workers
IX	14,15	Laborers

e. United States (including farm)
Source: Blau and Duncan (1967, p. 496)

I	1,2	Professionals
II	3,4	Managers and salesmen, not retail
III	5	Proprietors
IV	6,7	Clerical and retail sales
V	8,9 & 10	Craftsmen
VI	11,12	Operatives
VII	13	Service workers
VIII	14,15	Laborers
IX	16,17	Farm workers

Fig. 12. Sources of data for the international 9 x 9 tables and definitions of categories. (Roman numerals: our designation; arabic numbers: designation in source.)

The blockings used are illustrated in Figure 13. They are defined much as with the smaller tables. I is the full model of independence; D and U are the models for downward and upward mobility. Model Q is the blocking which includes both upward and downward movement, and has the maximum degrees of freedom consistent with Appendix 4. As such, Model Q is uniquely defined. With tables of this size, strong objection may be raised to blocking out so many cells and, as mentioned in Chapter 5, one may prefer the joint interpretation of models D and U to that of model Q.

FIGURE 13.

a. Model I: No cells blocked.

Number of free cells	= 81
Number of degrees of freedom	= 64
95%-ile of χ^2	= 78.0
99%-ile of χ^2	= 91.5

b. Model Q

X	X	X	X					
X	X	X	X					
X	X	X	X					
X	X	X	X					
				X				
					X	X	X	X
					X	X	X	X
					X	X	X	X
					X	X	X	X

Number of free cells	= 49
Number of degrees of freedom	= 31
95%-ile of χ^2	= 45.0
99%-ile of χ^2	= 52.2

c. *Model D*

X	X							
X	X							
X	X	X						
X	X	X	X					
X	X	X	X	X				
X	X	X	X	X	X			
X	X	X	X	X	X	X		
X	X	X	X	X	X	X	X	X
X	X	X	X	X	X	X	X	X

Number of free cells   = 34
Number of degrees of freedom = 21
95%-ile of χ^2 = 32.7
99%-ile of χ^2 = 38.9

d. *Model U*

X	X	X	X	X	X	X	X	X
X	X	X	X	X	X	X	X	X
		X	X	X	X	X	X	X
			X	X	X	X	X	X
				X	X	X	X	X
					X	X	X	X
						X	X	X
							X	X
							X	X

Number of free cells   = 34
Number of degrees of freedom = 21
95%-ile of χ^2 = 32.7
99%-ile of χ^2 = 38.9

Fig. 13. The basic 9 × 9 models. X indicates that a cell is blocked.

The tables are shown in the five panels of Table 27. Values of ϕ^2, e, Δ, and L are given in Table 28. Because there are only five tables and because they do not consistently include the farm category, it is not useful to consider rank correlations among the measures.

Our observations can be summarized as follows:

(1) The general ordering, in order of (quasi-) independence, is (a) United States, (b) Aarhus, (c) Puerto Rico, (d) Poona. This ordering holds over most models and measures, except that Aarhus and Puerto Rico are sometimes reversed in order.

(2) On Model I, Poona shows sharp departures from the model, relative to the other tables. Once the stayers are removed, however, and particularly with models D and U, Poona departs less from the pattern of the other tables.

(3) There is a small but consistent pattern of improvement in model I for the U.S. when the farm category is dropped. However, only the measure e shows a noticeable improvement for other models, viz. models Q and D, when the farm category is dropped.

TABLE 27.

Data and results for five international 9 × 9 tables

a. Aarhus, Denmark

Occupation of respondent

		I	II	III	IV	V	VI	VII	VIII	IX
	I	267	76	115	80	69	108	72	38	10
	II	94	73	56	46	88	95	71	26	6
	III	350	350	1763	712	300	1801	614	830	37
Occupation of father	IV	48	41	82	156	76	159	137	90	4
	V	15	10	20	28	30	33	35	20	0
	VI	144	175	534	326	198	2196	790	1141	26
	VII	78	91	224	139	130	533	326	257	13
	VIII	82	71	464	260	143	1536	781	2354	63
	IX	240	127	942	236	93	770	370	1014	138

119

Table 27 (Cont.)

b. Poona, India

Occupation of respondent

		I	II	III	IV	V	VI	VII	VIII	IX
	I	53	7	27	16	8	1	2	4	2
	II	31	116	20	20	29	17	6	16	12
Occupation of father	III	26	6	58	59	36	9	12	7	13
	IV	10	3	24	70	24	6	12	6	10
	V	2	7	11	19	165	10	14	7	15
	VI	13	52	8	37	33	151	19	30	34
	VII	11	15	42	62	74	23	111	37	49
	VIII	4	10	7	31	77	28	39	367	99
	IX	35	71	64	101	208	128	217	315	865

c. Puerto Rico (including farm)

Occupation of respondent

		I	II	III	IV	V	VI	VII	VIII	IX
	I	9	7	14	7	1	2	1	0	5
	II	13	16	9	9	11	11	9	3	1
Occupation of father	III	12	20	47	27	20	20	44	10	18
	IV	5	5	8	12	7	7	9	0	3
	V	3	12	16	9	58	22	32	16	8
	VI	3	1	3	9	17	26	13	8	4
	VII	6	7	13	5	20	27	33	11	14
	VIII	1	1	5	1	9	10	10	14	0
	IX	22	39	113	55	83	101	233	43	167

120

d. United States (farm not included)

Occupation of respondent

Occupation of father	I	II	III	IV	V	VI	VII	VIII	IX
I	669	325	80	113	28	142	168	50	32
II	539	629	183	149	43	275	142	34	33
III	496	687	455	175	94	360	248	80	49
IV	323	215	64	111	16	195	106	70	35
V	97	154	77	43	18	83	93	31	22
VI	815	771	469	487	93	1843	1098	323	302
VII	612	444	345	348	81	1250	1358	311	395
VIII	164	188	103	154	33	341	340	180	102
IX	130	142	81	177	34	498	582	201	313

e. United States (including farm)

Occupation of respondent

Occupation of father	I	II	III	IV	V	VI	VII	VIII	IX
I	669	325	80	141	142	168	50	32	26
II	539	629	183	192	275	142	34	33	19
III	496	687	455	269	360	248	80	49	43
IV	420	369	141	188	278	199	101	57	31
V	815	771	469	580	1843	1098	323	302	73
VI	612	444	345	429	1250	1358	311	395	98
VII	164	188	103	187	341	340	180	102	21
VIII	130	142	81	211	498	582	201	313	52
IX	525	583	719	606	2068	2196	577	937	2259

Upon closer examination, this result with e is due mainly to the relatively very small amount of movement into the farm category, which magnifies relative errors, as mentioned in Section 6.3. We conclude that for the United States, only model I is affected by presence or absence of the farm category, given that the number of categories is kept constant. Such a finding differs from an earlier study which indicated that the farm and non-farm populations had different supply and demand parameters in a small number of non-U.S. tables considered (Wiley, 1966).

(4) We note here a pattern common to most of the groups of

TABLE 28.

ϕ^2, e, Δ and L for the five international 9×9 tables.

	Model			
	I	Q	D	U
Measure: ϕ^2				
Aarhus	0.238	0.067	0.048	0.092
Poona	0.963	0.104	0.097	0.126
Puerto Rico (farm)	0.244	0.093	0.115	0.045
United States	0.192	0.028	0.020	0.027
United States (farm)	0.280	0.023	0.027	0.021
Measure: e				
Aarhus	0.589	0.375	0.436	0.294
Poona	0.963	0.299	0.294	0.377
Puerto Rico (farm)	0.593	0.404	0.384	0.307
United States	0.404	0.146	0.164	0.167
United States (farm)	0.460	0.210	0.264	0.157
Measure: Δ				
Aarhus	0.172	0.098	0.063	0.123
Poona	0.317	0.108	0.107	0.109
Puerto Rico (farm)	0.170	0.102	0.120	0.067
United States	0.168	0.059	0.056	0.062
United States (farm)	0.187	0.065	0.053	0.061
Measure: L				
Aarhus	0.790	0.816	0.844	0.820
Poona	–	0.838	0.830	0.832
Puerto Rico (farm)	0.761	0.806	0.811	0.821
United States	0.795	0.908	0.918	0.893
United States (farm)	0.782	–	0.915	0.912

tables of this and the preceding chapters: namely, that L shows far less variability than ϕ^2 and e. The contrast in level of variability is perhaps strongest with the present group of tables, and the reader might conclude that L does not discriminate well between tables and is, therefore, less useful than, say, ϕ^2. But recall that ϕ^2 is not normed and can easily exceed unity (and does so, for some earlier tables), even though it is less than unity for all of the present tables and models. L generally rank-correlates highly with ϕ^2, despite its smaller range. The range of L is greater than the range of Δ, on which it is based. And L is easily interpreted. We therefore accept L as justifiable evidence that

(5) the range in level of (quasi-) independence over a wide range in industrialization is extraordinarily narrow. The finding with smaller tables is supported. The subdivision of occupational categories, with its proliferation of mobility routes, does not bring out additional variation.

(6) The least expected finding is that for the countries considered in both 5×5 and 9×9 tables, the value of L is only slightly reduced in the larger table. More than three times as many routes are employed in each model, but L is reduced by only about 8 per cent or less for Poona, Puerto Rico, and the United States. In contrast, the unstandardized Δ varies considerably between the 5×5 and 9×9 tables. The main reason why $L = 1 - \Delta/\Delta_{max}$ changes little is that while Δ is larger for the larger tables, Δ_{max} is also larger. The marginal constraints have less effect on the interior of the table as the number of degrees of freedom increases. Although not developed with such a goal, it appears that Δ_{max} serves partly as a correction for aggregation or disaggregation.

(7) The pattern of errors on these tables is such that for models I, D, and U, there is consistent over-prediction of the number of distant moves. Thus, as before, there is a "distance" effect for those persons who do not move randomly. On Model Q, no such pattern to the errors emerges. This result is due to the groups of cells blocked by the Q model. The Q model, especially in large tables, is less a partitioning into mover and stayer subpopulations and more a partitioning into "exchange" and "nonexchange" sub-populations. As illustrated in Figure 13, the unblocked cells represent the exchange of persons between categories 1, 2, 3, 4, 5, on the one hand, and categories 5, 6, 7, 8, 9, on the other hand [except for the exclusion of cell (5, 5)]. We have two five-category clusters (with one category in common);

the unblocked cells describe movement *between* clusters but not *within* them (except for category 5). The U and D models are more consistent with the original mover-stayer motivation and are more strongly recommended for future work.

CHAPTER 8

Conclusions

Numerous suggestions have been made in this work for possible directions in which the present research can lead. In this brief chapter I shall emphasize what I believe are the most important directions.

(1) The improvement of the downward and upward quasi-perfect mobility models (D and U) over the full model of independence (I) implies that much of the impact of previous or father's occupation on present occupation is contained in the tripartite division of (a) moved up, (b) did not move, (c) moved down. Such a variable could be included in a regression analysis with "present SES" as dependent variable. (The three parts would require two dummy variables.) That is, if a difference of less than $\pm$ x SES points were considered evidence of no movement, then we could incorporate the tripartite variable rather than "previous SES" as an independent variable. My hypothesis is that the tripartite variable would explain nearly as much variation as does "previous SES".

(2) Goodman's multiplicative models permit us to quantify the "inertia" of each occupational group and the "barriers" between various groups. Results could be used to locate important gulfs or boundaries between major occupational groups. These quantities could also be related to SES differentials.

(3) Origin and destination effects (factors) for the quasi-perfect models could be further analysed. When the upward and downward models are considered separately, two sets of origin factors and two sets of destination factors are computed. If there are J groups, then for J–2 (the first and last excluded) of them there will be four factors. These can be arranged in a 2 x 2 x (J–2)

table (origin—destination vs. direction of move vs. occupational group). We could treat this table as an analysis of variance layout, for example, with one observation per cell (for testing purposes it would be necessary to make rather strong assumptions about error distributions). Then we could compute main effects for origin, direction, and occupation. Alternatively, the $2 \times 2 \times (J-2)$ table could be tested for first-order interaction and the $J-2$ origin-specific zero-order interactions could be compared. The pattern of values of these interactions as we proceed from occupation 2 to occupation $J-1$ could help identify "natural" ways of collapsing categories.

(4) Much has been written on comparability problems in cross-national comparison of mobility tables. We have described several ways of evaluating the importance of this issue for multiplicative models. Sensitivity of such models to the deletion of certain categories of high, intermediate, or low status (such as the farm category) could be handled similarly. If these models are not sensitive to combination and deletion choices, then any arbitrariness in such choices becomes less of an issue.

(5) The adjustment procedure of Chapter 4, which partially removes the effects of distributional change and differential fertility, could be used for a kind of cross-national comparison different from that of Chapter 7, but using largely the same data. The additional data required would be category-specific birth rates for the generation of fathers and for the same categories used in the mobility study (this comparability is often not possible). The model of Chapter 4 then permits cross-national comparisons of departures from "stable" movement for the various mobility routes.

(6) We have taken the occupational distributions at origin and destination times as given. It would be possible to locate these vectors in a large economic structure, using perhaps the technique of multivariate regression, in which all variables have a vector format. The occupation vector could be regressed on class-specific education levels, income levels, prestige levels, etc., for a series of countries, using comparable definitions of strata. The distribution vector could be used in other relations with economic variables and vectors.

(7) Measures of the level of quasi-independence can also be related at an ecological level to mean levels of education, income, GNP, etc., cross-nationally.

(8) Actual computation of the matrix of expected eventual

reproductive values each occupational group has for each other occupational group should be undertaken as soon as adequate data are available.

(9) The general log-linear model permits incorporation of additional variables in the analysis of cross-classified data. Some of the previous work can be extended to the case where education of son and of father, for example, are added to an inter-generational table.

(10) Multiplicative models, such as quasi-independence, could more readily be extended to the incorporation of other categorical variables. For example, we could deal with the three-way table of father's job vs. respondent's first job vs. respondent's present job. Quasi-independence could be evaluated for four mobile sub-populations: those who move up and up, up and down, down and up, down and down. One could also consider special four-way tables, in which movement is through lattices rather than just categories. For example, we could use a person's location at two time points in the two-way grid of occupation vs. region of the country. By appropriate choice of parameters we could articulate geographical and occupational mobility.

Similar directions can easily be proposed, and other suggestions appear in earlier chapters. It is most important to note that most of the work and suggestions of this research can be extended to other kinds of data and problems. These can include changes in political identity, region of residence, attitude, group membership, etc. Most sociological variables are, by nature, categorical, and in part this research has been an effort to illustrate methods which are powerful but are rarely used by sociologists.

The branching process framework

A. General theory

Here we present the relevant definitions and results from the general theory of branching processes. Suppose we have K types of objects, and at time t the number of objects of type i is z_t^i. Define the column vector Z_t by

$$Z_t = [z_t^i] \quad (i = 1, 2, \ldots, K)$$

The process $Z_0, Z_1, \ldots$ is a multi-type Galton-Watson process if

(1) the process is Markovian, i.e.,

$$\Pr(Z_t = X | Z_{t-1}, \ldots, Z_0) = \Pr(Z_t = X | Z_{t-1}),$$

(2) the process is time-independent, i.e.,

$$\Pr(Z_t = X | Z_{t-1}, \ldots, Z_0) = \Pr(Z_t = X | Z_{t-1}),$$

for all t_1 and $t_2 > 0$, and

(3) if $Z_0 = e_j$, the j-th column of the K × K identity matrix, then Z_1 has the generating function

$$f^j(s_1, \ldots, s_K) = \Sigma_{r_1, \ldots, r_K = 0}^{\infty} p^j(r_1, \ldots, r_K) s_1^{r_1} \ldots s_K^{r_K}, \text{ where}$$

$|s_1|, \ldots, |s_K| \leqslant 1$. Here $p^j(r_1, \ldots, r_K)$ is the probability that an object of type j has r_1 children of type 1, $\ldots$ r_K children of type K. If $z_t^j = r_j$, $j = 1, \ldots, K$, then Z_{t+1} is the sum of $r_1 + \ldots + r_K$ independent random vectors, r_1 having the generating function $f^1, \ldots, r_K$ having the generating function f^K (Harris, 1963, p. 36).

We now define some quantities which will appear frequently. $M = |m_{ij}|$ is the matrix of first moments of the process. The columns of M are given by $E(Z_1 | Z_0 = e_j)$, where e_j is the j-th column of the $K \times K$ identity matrix. Also, $V_j = \text{Cov}(Z_1 | Z_0 = e_j)$ and $C_t = E(Z_t Z_t')$. The following results are obtained directly from the definition of the process.

Result 1.

$$E(Z_{t+1} | Z_t) = E(Z_{t+1} | Z_t = \Sigma e_k (e_k' Z_t))$$

$$= \Sigma E(Z_{t+1} | Z_t = e_k \ (e_k' Z_t))$$

$$= \Sigma E(Z_{t+1} | Z_t = e_k)(e_k' Z_t)$$

$$= \Sigma E(Z_1 | Z_0 = e_k)(e_k' Z_t)$$

$$= M \, Z_t \, .$$

Result 2.

$$\text{Cov}(Z_{t+1} | Z_t) = \text{Cov}(Z_{t+1} | Z_t = \Sigma e_k (e_k' Z_t))$$

$$= \Sigma \text{Cov}(Z_{t+1} | Z_t = e_k (e_k' Z_t))$$

$$= \Sigma \text{Cov}(Z_{t+1} | Z_t = e_k)(e_k' Z_t)$$

$$= \Sigma \text{Cov}(Z_1 | Z_0 = e_k) z_t^k$$

$$= \Sigma V_k z_t^k \, .$$

Result 3.

$$C_{t+1} = E(Z_{t+1} Z_{t+1}') = E[E(Z_{t+1} Z_{t+1}' | Z_t)$$

$$= E[\text{Cov}(Z_{t+1} | Z_t) + E(Z_{t+1} | Z_t) E(Z_{t+1} | Z_t)']$$

$$= \Sigma V_k E(z_t^k) + M C_t M',$$

by Results 1 and 2. Repeated application gives

$$C_t = \Sigma_{j=1}^t M^{t-j} [\Sigma_{k=1}^K V_k E(z_{j-1}^k)(M^{t-j})' + M^t C_0 (M^t)'] .$$

But

$$E(Z_t) E(Z_t)' = M^t E(Z_0) E(Z_0)'(M^t)' = M^t E(Z_0 Z_0')(M^t)'$$

$$= M^t C_0 (M^t)',$$

since Z_0 is non-random and $Cov(Z_0) = E(Z_0 Z_0') - E(Z_0) E(Z_0)' = 0$. Hence

$$Cov(Z_t) = C_t - E(Z_t) E(Z_t)' = \Sigma_{j=1}^t M^{t-j} [\Sigma_{k=1}^K V_k E(z_{j-1}^k)] (M^{t-j})'.$$

Note that we can also write

$$Cov(Z_t) = \Sigma_{j=1}^t M^{t-j} \Sigma_{k=1}^K V_k e_k M^{j-1} Z_0 (M^{t-j})' .$$

Result 4.

$$E(Z_t) = E[E(Z_t|Z_{t-1})] = E(MZ_{t-1}) = ME(Z_{t-1}) = \ldots = M^t Z_0 .$$

Result 5.

In general, if M is a $K \times K$ matrix having a positive strictly dominant latent root λ of multiplicity one, with corresponding right and left latent vectors x and y', then it is possible to choose x and y' such that $y'x = 1$. Then for large values of t, $M^t/\lambda^t = xy' + R(t)$, where for a given θ, $0 < \theta < 1$, each entry of R(t) is of the order of $t^{K-2}\theta^t$ or smaller. Thus $\lim_{t \to \infty}(M^t/\lambda^t) = xy' = M_*$. This result, due to J. H. Pollard (1966), is more general than the older result for positively regular matrices, since a positively regular matrix always has a strictly dominant latent root of multiplicity one which is positive. Result 5 is given without proof.

We can interpret x in the general situation as follows. Since

$$Z_t = M^t Z_0,$$

$$\lim_{t \to \infty}(Z_t/\lambda^t) = \lim_{t \to \infty}(M^t Z_0/\lambda^t) = M_* Z_0 = xy' Z_0 = (y' Z_0)x,$$

y'Z being a scalar. Therefore x is proportional to the limit of Z_t after the main growth effect of λ has been taken out. Accordingly

131

x can be called the stable distribution vector. It is often standardized so that its topmost entry has the value 1.

To interpret y, recall the definition of M as the matrix whose columns are $E(Z_1|Z_0 = e_j)$, or, since the process is first order Markovian, $E(Z_{t+1}|Z_t = e_j)$. Hence the j-th column of M is the expected distribution of immediate descendants of a single person of type j. M_* can be expressed as the matrix whose j-th column is $E[\lim_{t\to\infty}(Z_t/\lambda^t)|Z_0 = e_j]$. But $M_* = xy' = (y_1 x, \ldots, y_k x)$, where $y' = (y_1, \ldots, y_k)$; i.e., the j-th column of M_* is $y_j x$. Therefore $y_j x$ is the expected *eventual* distribution of descendants of a single initial person of type j after the main growth effect of λ has been taken out. If the x vector is standardized so its topmost element is 1, then, for example, the top row of M_* will be $(y_1 \ldots y_k)$. We can therefore define y_j as the expected reproductive value of a person of type j for an eventual descendant of type 1, after the main growth effect of λ has been taken out, and $y_j x_i$ will be his expected reproductive value for type i. The standardization of y so that $y'x = 1$, i.e., $\Sigma y_j x_j = 1$, means that the sum of the expected reproductive values of one person of each type, each for his own respective type, is unity. This interpretation of y is due to Goodman (1968b).

Result 6.

Here we sketch the proof of the asymptotic result for the covariance matrix. We require $\lambda > 1$, λ defined as above.

$$\text{Cov}(Z_t/\lambda^t) = \lambda^{-2t}\text{Cov}(Z_t) = (1/\lambda^2)\Sigma_{j=1}^t (M^{t-j}/\lambda^{t-j})$$

$$\times [\Sigma_{k=1}^K V_k e_k (M^{j-1}/(\lambda^2)^{j-1})Z_0] \cdot (M^{t-j}/\lambda^{t-j})'$$

$$= (1/\lambda^2)\Sigma_{j=1}^t \Sigma_{k=1}^K (M^{t-j}/\lambda^{t-j}) V_k e_k (M/\lambda^2)^{j-1} Z_0$$

$$\times (M^{t-j}/\lambda^{t-j})'.$$

Clearly the sum will be finite for all t, for $\lambda > 1 \Rightarrow \lambda^2 > \lambda$ $\Rightarrow (M/\lambda^2)^{j-1} \to 0$, and convergence follows by comparison with the geometric series with parameter 2. Roughly speaking, the proof proceeds as follows: for small (finite) j, M^{t-j} converges to M_* as $t \to \infty$; for large j, $[M_* - (M^{t-j}/\lambda^{t-j})](M/\lambda^2)^{j-1}$ will be near 0. Hence we can write

$$\text{Cov}(Z_t/\lambda^t) = (1/\lambda^2)M_*[\Sigma_{j=1}^t \Sigma_{k=1}^K V_k e_k (M/\lambda^2)^{j-1}]M_*' + R(t)$$

$$= (1/\lambda^2)M_*[\Sigma_{k=1}^{K}V_k e_k \Sigma_{j=1}^{t}(M/\lambda^2)^{j-1}]M_*' + R(t)$$

$$= (1/\lambda^2)M_*[\Sigma_{k=1}^{K}V_k e_k (I - (M/\lambda^2))^{-1}]M_*' + R(t)$$

$$= M_*[\Sigma_{k=1}^{K}V_k e_k (\lambda^2 I - M)^{-1}]M_*' + R(t)$$

It can be shown that $R(t)$ is $0(\theta^t)$, $0 < \theta < 1$, whence

$$\lim_{t \to \infty}\mathrm{Cov}(Z_t/\lambda^t) = M_*[\Sigma_{k=1}^{K}V_k e_k (\lambda^2 I - M)^{-1}]M_*' .$$

For details see Harris (1951).

B. Variance-covariance structure of the labor force transition matrix of Section 2.2

Let e_k denote the k-th column of the $(I + K + 1)^2$ identity matrix, ranging from $k = 0$ through $k = K + I$. Define

$$V_k = \begin{pmatrix} V_{00k} & V_{01k} \\ V_{10k} & V_{11k} \end{pmatrix}$$

to be the $(I + K + 1)^2$ variance-covariance matrix of n_1 given that $n_0 = e_k$. The remaining notation is that of Section 2.2, except that $x(\mathrm{age})$ is replaced by k (the age and entry status index).

Straightforward computation gives

$$E[n_{11}(k + 1)|n_0 = e_k] = E[n_{11}(k + 1)|n_{00}(k) = 1] = h(k)$$

$$E[n_{11}^2(k + 1)|n_0 = e_k] = h(k)$$

$$E[n_{01}(k + 1)|n_0 = e_k] = E[n_{01}^2(k + 1)|n_0 = e_k] = a(k)$$

$$E[n_{01}(k + 1)\cdot n_{11}(k + 1)|n_0 = e_k] = h(k)a(k)$$
for $k = 0, \ldots, K$

and

$$E[n_{11}(k + 1)|n_0 = e_k] = E[n_{11}^2(k + 1)|n_0 = e_k] = m(k)$$

$$E[n_{01}(0)|n_0 = e_k] = b(k)$$

133

$$E[n_{01}^2(0)|n_0 = e_k] = \Sigma_i i^2 \phi_{i.}(k)$$

$$E[n_{11}(k+1) \cdot n_{01}(0)|n_0 = e_k] = \Sigma_i i \phi_{i_1}(k)$$

$$\text{for } k = K+1, \ldots, K+I$$

Let $V_{\alpha\beta k} = |v_{ij}^{\alpha\beta}(k)|$. $\alpha = 0$ or 1; $\beta = 0$ or 1.

Then, for $k = 0, \ldots, K$,

$$v_{ij}^{11}(k) = h(k)[1 - h(k)] \quad \text{if } (i, j) = (k+1, k+1)$$

$$\text{for } i = 1, \ldots, I \text{ and } j = 1, \ldots, I;$$

$$v_{ij}^{01}(k) = h(k)a(k)[1 - h(k)a(k)] \text{ if } (i, j) = (k+1, k+1)$$

$$\text{for } i = 0, \ldots, K \text{ and } j = 1, \ldots, I;$$

$$v_{ij}^{00}(k) = a(k)[1 - a(k)] \quad \text{if } (i, j) = (k+1, k+1)$$

$$\text{for } i = 0, \ldots, K \text{ and } j = 0, \ldots, K.$$

Turning to the post-entry categories $k = K+1, \ldots, K+I$, with ages $k' = k - K$, we have

$$v_{ij}^{11}(k) = m(k')[1 - m(k')] \text{ if } (i, j) = (k'+1, k'+1)$$

$$\text{for } i = 1, \ldots, I \text{ and } j = 1, \ldots, I;$$

$$v_{ij}^{01}(k) = \Sigma_i i \phi_{i_1}(k') - b(k') m(k') \text{ if } (i, j) = (0, k'+1)$$

$$\text{for } i = 0, \ldots, K \text{ and } j = 1, \ldots, I;$$

$$v_{ij}^{00}(k) = \Sigma i^2 \phi_1.(k') - b(k')^2 \text{ if } (i, j) = (0, 0)$$

$$\text{for } i = 0, \ldots, K \text{ and } j = 0, \ldots, K.$$

Because V_k must be symmetric, we also have $v_{ij}^{10}(k) = v_{ji}^{01}(k)$ for all age-entry status categories k. All entries not otherwise specified are zero.

Thus

$$\text{Cov}(n_t) = \Sigma_{j=1}^t A_{IK}^{t-j}(\Sigma_{k=0}^{I+K} V_k e_k n_{j-1})(A_{IK}^{t-j})',$$

with n_t, A_{IK}, and V_k defined as above.

134

To obtain the asymptotic results, we need λ, the principal latent root; x, the corresponding right latent vector; and y', the left latent vector. The roots of $|A_{IK} - \lambda\tilde{I}| = 0$ can be found, through induction, to be $\lambda = 0$, with multiplicity K, and the I + 1 roots of

(*) $\lambda = \Sigma_{i=1}^{I} b(i) c(i)/\lambda^i$,

where c(i) is defined by

$c(i) = \Sigma_{k=0}^{i-1} h(k) \ [\Pi_{j=k+1}^{i-1} m(j)] \ [\Pi_{j=0}^{k-1} a(j)]$,

$i = 1, \ldots, I$,

with

$\Pi_{i'=\alpha}^{\beta} \gamma(i') = 1$ if $\beta < \alpha$, by convention, and where $\tilde{I}$ denotes the $(I + K + 1)^2$ identity matrix.

Since the left hand side of the equation for λ is a strictly increasing function of λ and the right hand side is a strictly decreasing function of λ, (*) must have a positive, strictly dominant root of multiplicity 1. We can therefore continue with the asymptotic results. Let x and y' be the right (column) and left (row) latent vectors associated with λ. Specifically, $x = [x_\alpha(\beta)]$ and $y = [y_\alpha(\beta)]$, with $\alpha = 0$ and $\beta = 0, 1, \ldots, K$, followed by $\alpha = 1$ and $\beta = 1, 2, \ldots, I$; also $y_0(K) = 0$. Then, for example, in the case of $I = 3$, $K = 3$, we find

$x_0(1) = a(0)/\lambda$	$x_0(0) = 1$	$x_1(1) = c(1)/\lambda$
$x_0(2) = a(0)a(1)/\lambda^2$		$x_1(2) = c(2)/\lambda^2$
$x_0(3) = a(0)a(1)a(2)/\lambda^3$		$x_1(3) = c(3)/\lambda^3$.

Here $x_0(0)$ is arbitrarily set at 1. If $y_0(0) = \lambda/\psi_3$, where

$\psi_3 = 2b(1)c(1)/\lambda \ + \ 3b(2)c(2)/\lambda^2 \ + \ 4b(3)c(3)/\lambda^3$,

then $y'x = 1$ and

$y_0(1) = (1/\psi_3)\{a(1)h(2)b(3)/\lambda^2 + h(1) \ [b(2) + (m(2)b(3)/\lambda)]\}$

$$y_0(2) = (1/\psi_3)\, h(2)b(3)/\lambda$$

$$y_1(1) = (1/\psi_3)\, [b(1) + (m(1)/\lambda)\,(b(2) + [m(2)b(3)/\lambda])]$$

$$y_1(2) = (1/\psi_3)\, [b(2) + (m(2)b(3)/\lambda)]$$

$$y_1(3) = (1/\psi_3)\, b(3)$$

In general, if we set $x_0(0) = 1$ and $y_0(0) = \lambda/\psi_I$, where

$$\psi_I = \Sigma_{i=1}^{I}\, (i+1)b(i)c(i)/\lambda^i\ ,$$

then we will have $y'x = 1$ and

$$x_0(i) = d(i)/\lambda^i, \qquad i = 1, \ldots, K$$

$$x_1(i) = c(i)/\lambda^i, \qquad i = 1, \ldots, I$$

where we define

$$d(i) = \Pi_{j=0}^{i-1}\, a(j);$$

and

$$y_0(i) = [\lambda^i/\psi_I d(i)]\, \left\{ \Sigma_{j=i+1}^{I} b(j)c(j)/\lambda^j - [(c(i)m(i)/d(i)\lambda]\, y_1(i+1) \right\},$$
$$i = 1, \ldots, K-1$$

$$y_0(K) = 0$$

$$y_1(i) = (\lambda^0/\psi_I f(i))\, \Sigma_{j=i}^{I} b(j)f(j)/\lambda^j,$$
$$i = 1, \ldots, I$$

where we define

$$f(i) = \Pi_{j=1}^{i-1}\ m(j).$$

The above equations are easily obtained by induction from the recursive relationships illustrated with the case of $I = 3$ and $K = 3$. Here the elements of y are expressed in partially recursive form only to simplify computation, not to indicate any particular inter-relationships in the y-vector. We interpret x as the eventual age distribution over the pre- and post-entry categories, standardized on the 0-th age interval of the pre-entry category. We interpret $y_\delta(i)$ as the expected eventual reproductive value of a person in the pre-entry ($\delta = 0$) or post-entry ($\delta = 1$) category and age group i, for a person in the 0-th age group of the pre-entry category.

The asymptotic result for the covariance matrix is obtained immediately from Result 6 of Part A and from A_{IK}, $A_{IK*} \equiv xy'$, λ, and V_k as

$$\lim_{t \to \infty} \text{Cov}(n_t/\lambda^t) = A_{IK*} \left[\Sigma_{k=1}^{I+K+1} V_k e_k (\lambda^2 \tilde{I} - A_{IK})^{-1} \right] A_{IK*}$$

where $\tilde{I}$ denotes the $(I + K + 1)^2$ identity matrix.

137

APPENDIX 2

Asymptotic results for the discrete-time mobility model

A. We can easily apply the assumptions of the Galton-Watson process to the present model, employing the general techniques to obtain stochastic results. Computation of the V_k matrices (there are $J(I + K + 1)$ of them) required for both $Cov(n_t)$ and $\lim_{t \to \infty} Cov(n_t/\lambda^t)$, is straightforward but will not be discussed here. Rather, we proceed to $\lim_{t \to \infty} (A_{IKJ}^t/\lambda^t) = A_{IKJ*}$, for which we need λ, the dominant latent root, and x and y′, the right and left latent vectors.

The computation of λ will be discussed in Part B. The *existence* of the dominant latent root is conditional upon the quasi-positive regularity of A_{IKJ}. This condition will not be met if there are large numbers of transitions with zero probability, so that the B, M, and A submatrices are substantially zero off their main diagonals; I am unable to give a more precise statement. In practice, categories should be taken large enough so that zero cells in the B, M, and A submatrices are rare. Because large numbers of (narrowly defined) categories also induce computational difficulties and will be avoided, the condition should be easily met. It must be kept in mind that the following results depend on meeting this requirement. Express the right latent vector x of A_{IKJ} as in Appendix 1, except that the entries $x_\alpha(\beta)$ will now be $J \times 1$ column vectors themselves rather than scalars. In the same manner as in Appendix 1 we obtain by induction

$$x_0(k) = (D(k)/\lambda^k) \, x_0(0) \qquad \text{for } k = 1, \ldots, K$$

$$x_1(k) = (C(k)/\lambda^k) \, x_0(0) \qquad \text{for } k = 1, \ldots, I$$

where we define $D(k) = A(k - 1) \cdots A(0)$, and $C(k)$ is defined recursively by

$$C(1) = H(0)$$

$$C(k) = M(k - 1)C(k - 1) + H(k - 1)D(k - 1) \quad \text{for } k > 1.$$

Computation of x is thus simplified to computation of $x_0(0)$. Observe that x and $x_0(0)$ are in a one-to-one relationship; if we know one we can uniquely find the other. Because λ is assumed to have multiplicity one, its associated right latent vector, x, must lie in a manifold of dimension one in $R^{J(I+K+1)}$. That is, x is determined within a scalar multiple, and $A_{IKJ}x = \lambda x$ can be solved for x within a scalar multiple. By substituting the above values for $x_0(k)$ into this equation and utilizing the recursive definition of $C(k)$, it can be shown that the equation $A_{IKJ}x = \lambda x$ is equivalent to the equation $[\Sigma_{k=1}^{I} B(k)C(k)/\lambda^k] x_0(0) = \lambda x_0(0)$, in the sense that both can be solved within a scalar multiple. Therefore the system of J equations in $x_{01}(0), \ldots, x_{0J}(0)$ expressed by this single vector equation has a unique solution with $x_{01}(0) = 1$. (We are standardizing the x-vector, the eventual distribution vector, on the number of pre-entry persons of age 0 in occ. 1.) The suggested method of solution is iteration with $x_{01}(0)$ fixed at 1.

We express the left latent vector y' as the transpose of a vector y which is identical in form to x, except that each "x" in the symbol representation of x should be replaced by a "y", and $y_0(K) = 0$. We then obtain another set of equations similar to those of the labor force model. Here, however, instead of a partially recursive solution we give a fully recursive solution:

$$y_1(I) = (1/\lambda)B(I)'y_0(0)$$

and

$$y_1(k) = (1/\lambda)[B(k)'y_0(0) + M(k)'y_1(k + 1)], k = 1, \ldots, I - 1,$$

$$y_0(K-1) = (1/\lambda^2)H(I - 1)'B(1)'y_0(0)$$

and

$$y_0(k) = (1/\lambda)[A(k)y_0(K - 1) + H(k)'y_0(k + 1)],$$

139

$k = 2, \ldots, K - 2$.

Thus computation of y is simplified to computation of $y_0(0)$. However, similar to the result for the right latent vector,

$$[\Sigma_{k=1}^{I}\ B(k)C(k)/\lambda^k]\ 'y_0(0)\ =\ \lambda y_0(0).$$

By reasoning analagous to that just preceding, $y_0(0)$ can be determined iteratively if we fix $y_{01}(0) = 1$. Let $\tilde{y}_0(0)$ be the solution vector thus obtained. The final step is to standardize y (i.e., to standardize $y_0(0)$ so that $y'x = 1$. By substituting in the values of $x_0(k)$, $x_1(k)$, $y_0(k)$, $y_1(k)$, we can show that

$$y'x\ =\ y_0(0)'[\Sigma_{k=1}^{I}kB(k)C(k)/\lambda^{k+1}+\bar{I}]\,x_0(0)\ .$$

Thus, to standardize y we simply substitute $\tilde{y}_0(0)$ and $x_0(0)$ into this equation; the result will be $y'x = r$, a scalar. The standardized $y_0(0)$, which will satisfy $y'x = 1$, will then be given by $y_0(0) = (1/r)\tilde{y}_0(0)$. ($\bar{I}$ is the J x J identity matrix.)

Hence we have computed x, the age-occupation vector for the stable population, and y, the vector of expected reproductive values. Suppose now that we wished to compute the reproductive value of a post-entry person, age k, occ. j, for the post-entry category of age k', occ. j'. From the earlier discussion of reproductive values, this is found to be simply $y_{1j}(k)x_{1j'}(k')$. The reproductive value of a post-entry person, age k, occ. j, for the entire post-entry occ. group j' would be

$$y_{1j}(k)\ \Sigma_{k'=1}^{I}x_{1j'}(k').$$

The reproductive value of the entire post-entry occ. group j for the entire post-entry occ. group j' can be formulated as follows. Conceptually distribute one initial person in the first group over the I age categories of that group, and distribute that person according to the stable population distribution in that group. The quantity thus obtained will be referred to as $u_{jj'}$, the stably-adjusted reproductive value of group j for group j'.

Thus one person is distributed over group j so that $x_{1j}(k)/[\Sigma_{k=1}^{I}x_{1j}(k)]$ of an individual is in age group k of occ. j (here we are discussing only post-entry individuals). This fraction of a person has reproductive value

$$(x_{1j}(k)/\Sigma_{k=1}^{I}x_{1j}(k))\ y_{1j}(k)\ \Sigma_{k'=1}^{I}x_{1j'}(k')$$

for occupation j, and adding over the categories in occupation k, we obtain

$$u_{jj'} = \Sigma_{k=1}^I \Sigma_{k'=1}^I y_{1j}(k)x_{1j}(k)x_{1j'}(k')/\Sigma_{k=1}^I x_{1j}(k)$$

$u_{jj'}$ can be considered as a weighted average of the column totals in the (j', j) block of the matrix N_{IJ*}, where N_{IJ*} is obtained from $xy' = M_{IJ*}$ by rearranging the rows and columns of M_{IJ*} so that the lexicographic ordering is first by occupation and then by age, rather than first by age and then by occupation.

Let $U = |u_{jj'}|$ be the $J \times J$ matrix of stably-adjusted reproductive values of occupation j for occupation j'. The U matrix is suggested as a supplement, for some purposes of analysis, to the conventional mobility table in which sons are sampled and their own and their father's occupations are recorded. Because of the adjustments involved in this model it is believed that the U matrix may be a better indicator of such things as the relative nearness of occupations and the similarity of occupational mobility patterns than is the conventional table.

B. We now discuss the computation of the principal latent root, λ, which is the main growth factor. We shall also attempt to integrate the preceding discussion with Goodman's discussion of population growth (1969). In order to improve conformity with the various bodies of literature from which this appendix is drawn, we employ a notation more similar to that of the main part of this work than to the earlier appendix. Principally, the symbol "x" will again represent age, rather than the left latent vector. The symbols "p" and "y" will be used in connection with the age distribution and reproductive values, respectively, replacing "x" and "y" of the previous discussion. It is impossible, unfortunately, to find symbols with the same conventional usage in both mathematical demography and the theory of branching processes.

Let $p(x, j')$ be a $J \times 1$ column vector with elements $p(x, j', j)$ for $j = 1, \ldots, J$. We define $p(x, j', j)$ to be the probability that a person in the state at left below will *survive* to the state at right below:

time t	*time t + x*
pre-entry	post-entry
age group $\overline{0}$	age group $\overline{x}$
occ. group j	occ. group j'

Let $e(j)$ be the j-th column of the $J \times J$ identity vector, with all elements equal to zero except for the j-th element, which is equal to unity. We can think of $e(j)$ as representing the distribution of an initial group of pre-entry persons of age 0 when this group consists of a single individual in occupation j. The vector $p(x, j')$ will then be defined by

$$p(x, j') = \Sigma_{\alpha=1}^{\beta} \left\{ [\Pi_{z=\alpha+1}^{x-1} M(z)] \; H(\alpha) \; [\Pi_{y=0}^{\alpha-1} A(y)] \right\} e(j),$$

where $\beta = \min(x - 1, K - 1)$, and multiplication is from right to left. This definition holds for ages $x = 1, \ldots, I$. Thus, according to our model, a person starts in category j at age 0, and over x intervals of time he must survive within the pre-entry status (a sequence of A matrices), move into the post-entry status (a single H matrix), and survive (and move) within the post-entry status (a series of M matrices) in order to attain various occupations j' at age x.

Now, due to the ergodicity of the process, the eventual distribution does not depend on the original distribution, so that by starting with the origin distribution $e(j)$ we obtain, in a simple way, the same proportional distribution as if we started with an actual, observed initial distribution. Thus, regardless of the actual initial distribution, the asymptotic age-distribution of post-entry persons will be proportional to the vector

$$p_*(x, j') \equiv p(x, j')/\lambda^x$$

for $x = 1, \ldots, I$. Or, in scalar form,

$$p_*(x, j', j) \equiv p(x, j', j)/\lambda^x$$

for all x, j, and j'.

Only post-entry persons can produce sons, and the expected numbers of sons produced are given by B matrices. That is, as before, $b_{ij'}(x)$ is the (i, j') element of $B(x)$ and is the expected number of sons in the 0-th age interval and i-th class at time $t + 1$ born to a post-entry male in the x-th age interval and j'-th class at time t.

Therefore, in the stable population, the number of sons that a person age 0, pre-entry, and of occupation j can be expected to produce who will in turn be age 0, pre-entry, and of occupation i will be proportional to

$$\gamma_{ij} = \Sigma_{x=1}^{I} \Sigma_{j'=1}^{J} b_{ij'}(x) p_*(x, j', j).$$

This formula sums over all intervening occupations j' and over all reproductive ages x. Let P_* be proportional to the eventual expected distribution over occupations of pre-entry sons age 0. It is possible now to define the constant of proportionality for $p_*(x, j')$, for γ_{ij}, and for P_*, by the convention that the first element of P_* is unity. That is, all expected numbers are "per son of age 0 and occupation I."

The γ_{ij} define a matrix $\Gamma \equiv |\gamma_{ij}|$. For Γ as defined, we have $\Gamma P_* = \lambda P_*$, with λ related to Γ both via the definition of the γ_{ij} in terms of the $p_*(x, j', j)$, and via the characteristic equation $|\Gamma - \lambda I| = 0$. Here I and 0 are the $J \times J$ identity and zero matrices, respectively. This equation implies a polynomial with unknown λ.

By this general method, due to Goodman (1969, pp. 679–681) we are able to solve easily for the parameter λ, for the right latent vector P_* of Γ, and for the entire eventual age-occupational distribution, both pre- and post-entry. The expected number of post-entry persons of age x and occupation j' in the stable population, per person who is pre-entry, age 0, and of occupation 1, will be the scalar

$$\Sigma_{j=1}^{I} P_*(j) p_*(x, j', j).$$

Here we have summed over all origins j which can lead to j', weighting each by their origin frequency. The expected number of pre-entry persons of age x and occupation j' will be determined simply by survival to be the j'-th element of the vector

$$[\Pi_{y=0}^{x-1} A(y)] P_* / \lambda^x.$$

For numerical work, and perhaps for comprehension of the process, this method is far superior to the basically inductive and recursive method of part A of this appendix.

Similarly, the equation $V\Gamma = V\lambda$ will give the left latent vector of expected reproductive values. We may standardize the $1 \times J$ row vector V by setting its first element equal to unity. The j-th element in V will be $V(j')$, the expected reproductive value of a pre-entry male age 0 and class j' (relative to the unit value of class 1) for the eventual population.

The remaining reproductive values are then not difficult to obtain. Let $v(x)$ be the $1 \times J$ row whose j'-th element is the expected reproductive value of a post-entry person age x. Then

$$v(x) = c\Sigma_{j'=1}^{J} V(j') \left\{ \Sigma_{z=x}^{I} b_{j'}(z) \ [\Pi_{w=x}^{a-1} M(w)]/\lambda \right\} ,$$

where $b_{j'}(z)$ is a $1 \times J$ row vector, the j'-th row of $B(z)$. This formula is obtained, roughly speaking, by (a) partitioning the basic vector V into its distinct occupational groups j', and then recombining; (b) surviving persons through the post-entry ages by a product of M matrices; (c) for each possible age, computing expected births with a row of the appropriate B matrix; (d) dividing out the main effect, λ, and (e) including a constant c. By Goodman's general method, c will be given by

$$c = \lambda/\Sigma_{j'=1}^{J} V(j') \ [\Sigma_{x=1}^{I} (x+1)b_{j'}(x)P_*(x)] ,$$

where the $J \times 1$ column vector $P_*(x)$ is the eventual occupational distribution of post-entry persons age x. This quantity represents the reciprocal of the average age of child-bearing in the stable population.

The reproductive values of pre-entry persons are given by a simple alteration of these formulae (with c unchanged) in which we incorporate survival and inter-generational movement (the H matrix) required before reaching post-entry status. The formula for the pre-entry analog of $v(x)$ would agree with the formula for $v(x)$, with the difference that the term

$$[\Pi_{w=z}^{z-1} M(w)]$$

would be replaced by the term

$$\Sigma_{\alpha=1}^{\beta} \ [\Pi_{w=\alpha+1}^{z-1} M(w)] \ H(\alpha) \ [\Pi_{y=z}^{\alpha-1} A(y)]$$

where $\beta = \min(z-1, K-1)$.

Once these quantities have been computed, we are able to define the reproductive value of one occupation for another occupation exactly as in part A of this appendix (in equivalent symbols), leading to the matrix U defined therein.

Certain assumptions of this model, in particular the assumption that pre-entry persons do not have children, can be weakened rather easily under the general method utilized above.

There are two reasons why the model was not applied to actual data for this work. The first reason is the extensive computer programming time that would have been required, even for the formulas derived from the general method. The second reason is the unavailability of most of the data needed for an actual population. For all cohorts of men, we need (a) decennial mobility rates, (b) age-occupation-specific birth rates, (c) age and occupation at entry into the labor force, (d) occupation of father. By using cohorts from cross-sectional data and making numerous inferences and adjustments about data of types (b) and (c) we could have applied the model. However, so many adjustments, combinations of different sources of data, and assumptions would have been required that the application would be little more than a tedious exercise, with very low validity. The Blau-Duncan study could have been adapted if it had included information on, say, "occupation ten years ago".

The U matrix, as a summary of birth, death, and mobility rates at a point in time, is considered one of the major suggestions of this study. It is hoped that it can soon be computed using actual data.

APPENDIX 3

Program listing for the model of implied mobility

The following subroutine adjusts any rectangular input table to a table with desired marginals but with the same zero-order interactions as the input table. To be used, the subroutine must be accompanied by a main program which reads the number, size, and entries of the input table, and by subroutine WRITE2. The necessary statements, subroutine WRITE2, and the meanings of any critical parameters are specified in Appendix 5.

```
      SUBROUTINE ADJUST (NAME,IDIM,JDIM,IDIR,JDIR,TABLE)
C   THIS SUBROUTINE ADJUSTS TABLE ENTRIES TO OBTAIN DESIRED
C   MARGINALS WITH UNCHANGED INTERACTIONS
      ODIMENSION TABLE(18,18), ROWTOT(18), COLTOT(18), SETROW(18),
     1SETCOL(18), TEMP(18,18), TEMROW(18), TEMCOL(18), ROWRAT(18),
     2COLRAT(18), ABSROW(18)
      DIMENSION  ABSCOL(18)
   10 FORMAT (8F10.4)
  450 FORMAT ( //, 30X, 34HNO CONVERGENCE AFTER 50 ITERATIONS )
 2700FORMAT (1H1, 40X, 18HADJUSTED TABLE NO., I2, //, 30X,
     120HADJUSTMENT REQUIRED . I3,11H ITERATIONS, ///, 12X)
      DO 15 I=1,IDIM
   15 ROWTOT(I)=0.0
      DO 20 J=1,JDIM
   20 COLTOT(J)=0.0
      DO 25 I=1,IDIM
      DO 25 J=1,JDIM
      ROWTOT(I)=ROWTOT(I)+TABLE(I,J)
   25 COLTOT(J)=COLTOT(J)+TABLE(I,J)
      TOTAL=0.0
      DO 32 I=1,IDIM
   32 TOTAL=TOTAL+ROWTOT(I)
C OPTION TO USE PROVIDED, UNCHANGED, OR MATCHED MARGINALS AS IDIR=0,1
      IF(IDIR-1) 35,40,45
   35 RIT 5,10, (SETROW(I), I=1,IDIM)
      GO TO 50
   40 DO 42 I=1,IDIM
   42 SETROW(I)=ROWTOT(I)
      GO TO 50
   45 DO 47 I=1,IDIM
   47 SETROW(I)=COLTOT(I)
```

```
C OPTION TO USE PROVIDED, UNCHANGED, OR MATCHED MARGINALS AS JDIR=0,1,2
   50 IF(JDIR-1) 60,65,70
   60 RIT 5,10, (SETCOL(J), J=1,JDIM)
      GO TO 75
   65 DO 67 J=1,JDIM
   67 SETCOL(J)=COLTOT(J)
      GO TO 75
   70 DO 72 J=1,JDIM
   72 SETCOL(J)=ROWTOT(J)
   75 DO 80 I=1,IDIM
      DO 80 J=1,JDIM
   80 TEMP(I,J)=TABLE(I,J)
   82 DO 85 I=1,IDIM
   85 TEMROW(I)=0.0
      DO 95 I=1,IDIM
      DO 95 J=1,JDIM
   95 TEMROW(I)=TEMROW(I)+TEMP(I,J)
      ITERAT=0
C ITERATION BEGINS
   97 DO 105 I=1,IDIM
  105 ROWRAT(I)=SETROW(I)/TEMROW(I)
      DO 110 I=1,IDIM
      DO 110 J=1,JDIM
  110 TEMP(I,J)=TEMP(I,J)*ROWRAT(I)
      DO 120 J=1,JDIM
  120 TEMCOL(J)=0.0
      DO 125 J=1,JDIM
      DO 125 I=1,IDIM
  125 TEMCOL(J)=TEMCOL(J)+TEMP(I,J)
      TESTCO=0.0
      DO 126 J=1,JDIM
      ABSCOL(J)=ABSF(TEMCOL(J)-SETCOL(J))
  126 TESTCO=TESTCO+ABSCOL(J)
      DO 130 J=1,JDIM
  130 COLRAT(J)=SETCOL(J)/TEMCOL(J)
      DO 135 J=1,JDIM
      DO 135 I=1,IDIM
  135 TEMP(I,J)=TEMP(I,J)*COLRAT(J)
      DO 140 I=1,IDIM
  140 TEMROW(I)=0.0
      DO 145 I=1,IDIM
      DO 145 J=1,JDIM
  145 TEMROW(I)=TEMROW(I)+TEMP(I,J)
      DO 150 I=1,IDIM
  150 ABSROW(I)=ABSF(TEMROW(I)-SETROW(I))
      TESTRO=0.0
      DO 160 I=1,IDIM
  160 TESTRO=TESTRO+ABSROW(I)
      ITERAT=ITERAT+1
C THROW OFF IF MORE THAN 50 ITERATIONS
      IF(ITERAT-50) 161,161,400
  161 IF(TESTRO+TESTCO-.0001) 162,162,97
C ITERATION PROCEDURE FINISHED
  400 WOT 6,450
      GO TO 320
  162 WOT 6,270, NAME,ITERAT
      CALL WRITE2 (IDIM,JDIM,TEMP)
  320 RETURN
      END
```

APPENDIX 4

Constraints on quasi-perfect blockings

Let S be the set of all cells in a mobility table, and let Z and N be the subsets of S that are constrained and not constrained, respectively; then $S = Z \cup N$.

If quasi-independence holds then for all $(i, j) \epsilon N$, there are row effects $|a_i|$ and column effects $|b_j|$ such that $p_{ij} = a_i b_j$. Consequently, if R_{ij} is the Rogoff ratio of page 5 then for all $(i, j) \epsilon N$,

$$R_{ij} = \frac{p_{ij}}{p_{i.}p_{.j}} = \left(\frac{a_i}{p_{i.}} \right) \left(\frac{b_j}{p_{.j}} \right)$$

However, we have observed that for ordered categories, R_{ij} diminishes as we move toward cells representing the farthest moves. Thus for each fixed j, say, the sequence $|a_i/p_{i.}|$ must diminish as the quantity $|i - j|$ increases; similarly, for each fixed i the sequence $|b_j/p_{.j}|$ must diminish as the quantity $|i - j|$ increases.

There are only two reasonable blocking patterns with a mover-stayer interpretation which are consistent with such sequences. The first, which has been used in all mobility applications thus far, involves an expansion of the "stayers" to include persons who have made short moves, so that *not more than one* occupational group has unblocked cells in *both* the upwardly and downwardly mobile triangles of cells. That is, minimal blockings of stayers will constrain an a x a block, say, in the upper left, a b x b block, say, in the lower right of the table, and a single cell in the main diagonal, with a and b such that $a + b + 1 = J$, the number of strata.

If B is the number of blocked cells, the degrees of freedom of such a blocking will be $(J - 1)^2 - B = (a + b)^2 - a^2 - 1 - b^2 =$

2ab − 1. If J is odd, the minimal stayer blocking with most degrees of freedom has a = b, with $-1 + (J - 1)^2/2$ degrees of freedom. Table 3 illustrates such a case with J = 5. If J is even, the minimal stayer blocking with most degrees of freedom has |a − b| = 1, with $J(J - 2)/2 - 1$ degrees of freedom.

The second kind of plausible blocking retains only the upper triangle or lower triangle of the table. Later, these two triangles can be pooled to include *almost* all cells except the main diagonal.

Therefore, given prior knowledge that one's categories are ordered, the null hypothesis that quasi-independence obtains in a mobility table will be better defended by one or the other of these types of blocking, the second type of which makes more efficient use of the table's degrees of freedom.

APPENDIX 5

Program listing for the model of quasi-perfect mobility

The following Fortran II computer program performed the quasi-perfect (or quasi-independent) computations used in Chapters 6–7. In order to use it, one only need know that

IDIM = number of rows in table

JDIM = number of columns in table

NAME = table number

NBLOCK = blocking or model number

TABLE = input table

BLOCK = input blocking

Formatting of imput is clear from the first page, i.e., the main program. A code symbol, INIT, which must follow each blocking read into the machine, is defined in the main program.

```
C     THIS PROGRAM PERFORMS QUASI-PERFECT COMPUTATIONS
      DIMENSION TABLE(18,18), BLOCK(18,18)
  170 FORMAT(1H1,40X,16HINPUT TABLE NO. ,I3,///)
  180 FORMAT(1H1,12X,15HBLOCKING NUMBER,I3,16H LOOKS LIKE THIS,///)
 5000 FORMAT (3I2)
 5100 FORMAT (8F10.4)
 5010 FORMAT (80F1.0)
 5200 FORMAT (I1)
    2 RIT 5,5000,NAME,IDIM,JDIM
      WOT 6,170,NAME
      RIT 5,5100, ((TABLE(I,J),J=1,JDIM),I=1,IDIM)
      CALL WRITE2 (IDIM,JDIM,TABLE)
    1 RIT 5,5000,NBLOCK,IDIM,JDIM
C     BLOCK=1 MEANS CELL IS NOT BLOCKED, BLOCK=0 MEANS CELL IS BLOCKED
      RIT 5,5010, ((BLOCK(I,J), J=1,JDIM), I=1,IDIM)
      CALL QUASIP(NAME,IDIM,JDIM,NBLOCK,TABLE,BLOCK)
      RIT 5,5200,INIT
      GO TO (1,2,3),INIT
C     INIT=1 MEANS SAME TABLE, NEW BLOCKING, INIT=2 MEANS NEW TABLE,
C     INIT=3 MEANS END OF FILE
C     INIT MUST BE SPECIFIED AFTER EACH BLOCKING
    3 CALL EXIT
      END
```

```
      SUBROUTINE QUASIP (NAME,IDIM,JDIM,NBLOCK,TABLE,BLOCK)
      DIMENSION TABLE(17,17),BLOCK(17,17),HOLD(17,17)
      DIMENSION TEMP1(17,17),TEMP2(17,17),TEMP3(17,17)
      DIMENSION ROWTOT(17),COLTOT(17),ROWFQP(17),COLFQP(17),TEST1(17)
      DIMENSION TEST2(17),TEST3(17),TEST4(17),ERR(17),PRR(17)
      COMMON NEW,HOLD,BLOCK
  190 FORMAT(//,11X,15HROW FACTORS ARE,//,2X,9(E11.5,3X),//,2X,9(11.5,3X
     1),//)
  200 FORMAT(//,11X,15HCOL FACTORS ARE,//,2X,9(E11.5,3X),//,2X,9(11.5,3X
     1),//)
  210 FORMAT(1H1,9X,20HTHIS IS TABLE NUMBER ,I3,21H WITH BLOCKING NUMBER
     1,I3,3X,21H CONVERGENCE REQUIRED,I3,11H ITERATIONS,///)
  215 FORMAT (//,9X,42HTABLE OF RELATIVE DEPARTURES (OBS-EXP)/EXP,///)
  220 FORMAT (11X,20HAV ABS(OBS-EXP)/EXP,10X,19HCOEFF DISSIMILARITY,
     111X,10HCHI-SQUARE,20X,12HCORRELATION ,///)
  225 FORMAT (11X,F12.6,18X,F12.6,18X,F12.6,18X,F12.6,///)
  226 FORMAT (11X,15HUNBLOCKED TOTAL,15X,17HCOEFF CONTINGENCY,13X,3HPHI,
     127X,19HNO. UNBLOCKED CELLS,///)
 2270FORMAT (11X,67HAV ABS(OBS-EXP)/EXP AND AV (OBS-EXP)/EXP FOR DISTAN
     1CE FROM DIAGONAL,//)
  228 FORMAT (20X,F12.6,10X,F12.6,20X ,I2,//)
  230 FORMAT (1H1,26HTHE COMPLEMENTARY TABLE IS ,///)
      DO 5 I=1,IDIM
      DO 5 J=1,JDIM
    5 TEMP1(I,J)=TABLE(I,J)*BLOCK(I,J)
      DO 15 I=1,IDIM
   15 ROWTOT(I)=0.0
      DO 20 J=1,JDIM
   20 COLTOT(J)=0.0
      DO 25 I=1,IDIM
      DO 25 J=1,JDIM
      ROWTOT(I)=ROWTOT(I)+TEMP1(I,J)
   25 COLTOT(J)=COLTOT(J)+TEMP1(I,J)
      ITERAT=0
      DO 30 I=1,IDIM
   30 ROWFQP(I)=ROWTOT(I)
C     ITERATION BEGINS
   35 ITERAT=ITERAT+1
      IF(ITERAT-50) 40,40,105
   40 TOTAL=0.0
      DO 45 I=1,IDIM
   45 TOTAL=TOTAL+ROWFQP(I)
      DO 50 I=1,IDIM
      ROWFQP(I)=ROWFQP(I)/TOTAL
   50 TEST1(I)=ROWFQP(I)
      TUST=0.0
      DO 70 J=1,JDIM
      DENJ=0.0
      DO 55 I=1,IDIM
   55 DENJ=DENJ+BLOCK(I,J)*ROWFQP(I)
      IF(DENJ)   60,60,65
   60 COLFQP(J)=0.0
      GO TO 67
   65 COLFQP(J)=COLTOT(J)/DENJ
   67 TEST3(J)= ABSF(COLFQP(J)-TEST4(J))
      TUST=TUST+TEST3(J)
   70 TEST4(J)=COLFQP(J)
      TEST=0.0
      DO 85 I=1,IDIM
      DENI=0.0
      DO 75 J=1,JDIM
   75 DENI=DENI+BLOCK(I,J)*COLFQP(J)
      IF(DENI)   80,80,85
   80 ROWFQP(I)=0.0
      GO TO 90
   85 ROWFQP(I)=ROWTOT(I)/DENI
   90 TEST2(I)=ABSF(ROWFQP(I)-TEST1(I))
```

151

```
    95 TEST=TEST+TEST2(I)
       IF(TEST+TOST-.0001) 105,105,35
C      ITERATION ENDS
   105 TOTAL=0.0
       DO 120 I=1,IDIM
       DO 120 J=1,JDIM
       IF(BLOCK(I,J))        110,110,115
   110 TEMP1(I,J)=0.0
       GO TO 120
   115 TEMP1(I,J)=ROWFQP(I)*COLFQP(J)
       TOTAL=TOTAL+TEMP1(I,J)
   120 CONTINUE
       WOT 6,210,NAME,NBLOCK,ITERAT
       CALL WRITE2 (IDIM,JDIM,TEMP1)
       WOT 6,190, (ROWFQP(I),I=1,IDIM)
       WOT 6,200,(COLFQP(J),J=1,JDIM)
       DISSIM=0.0
       ER=0.0
       CHI=0.0
       D1=0.0
       D2=0.0
       TOP=0.0
       COUNT=0.0
       DO 130 I=1,IDIM
       DO 130 J=1,JDIM
       IF (BLOCK(I,J)) 127,127,125
   125 TEMP3(I,J)=TABLE(I,J)-TEMP1(I,J)
       CHI=CHI+(TEMP3(I,J)**2   )/TEMP1(I,J)
       DISSIM=DISSIM+ABSF(TEMP3(I,J))/(TOTAL*2.0)
       TEMP3(I,J)=TEMP3(I,J)/TEMP1(I,J)
       ER=ER+ABSF(TEMP3(I,J))
       D1=D1+(TEMP1(I,J)**2   )
       D2=D2+(TABLE(I,J)**2   )
       TOP=TOP+TEMP1(I,J)*TABLE(I,J)
       COUNT=COUNT+1.0
       GO TO 130
   127 TEMP3(I,J)=0.0
   130 CONTINUE
       WOT 6,215
       CALL WRITE1 (IDIM,JDIM,TEMP3)
       ER=ER/COUNT
       TOP=TOP-(TOTAL**2)/COUNT
       D1=D1-(TOTAL**2)/COUNT
       D2=D2-(TOTAL**2)/COUNT
       CORR=TOP/SQRTF(D1*D2)
       PHI=CHI/TOTAL
       COCON=SQRTF(PHI/(1.0+PHI))
       WOT 6,220
       WOT 6,225,ER,DISSIM,CHI,CORR
       WOT 6,226
       WOT 6,225,TOTAL,COCON,PHI,COUNT
       FLOAT=0.0
       ED=0.0
       PD=0.0
       KDIL=XMINOF(IDIM-1,JDIM-1)
       DO 1343 I=1,KDIL
       IF (BLOCK(I,I)) 1343,1343,1342
  1342 ED=ED+ABSF(TEMP3(I,I))
       PD=PD+TEMP3(I,I)
       FLOAT=FLOAT+1.0
  1343 CONTINUE
       FLOAT=MAX1F(FLOAT,1.0)
       ED=ED/FLOAT
       PD=PD/FLOAT
       LZERO=0
       WOT 6,227
       WOT 6,228,ED,PD,LZERO
```

152

```
       KDIM=XMAXOF(IDIM-1,JDIM-1)
       DO 134 K=1,KDIM
       ERR(K)=0.0
       PRR(K)=0.0
       FLOAT=0.0
       DO 133 I=1,IDIM
       DO 133 J=1,JDIM
       IF(BLOCK(I,J)) 133,133,131
  131  L=K-XABSF(I-J)
       IF(L) 133,132,133
  132  ERR(K)=ERR(K)+ABSF(TEMP3(I,J))
       PRR(K)=PRR(K)+TEMP3(I,J)
       FLOAT=FLOAT+1.0
  133  CONTINUE
       FLOAT=MAX1F(FLOAT,1.0)
       PRR(K)=PRR(K)/FLOAT
  134  ERR(K)=ERR(K)/FLOAT
       DO 1345 K=1,KDIM
 1345  WOT 6,228,ERR(K),PRR(K),K
       DO 145 I=1,IDIM
       DO 145 J=1,JDIM
       IF (BLOCK(I,J)) 135,135,140
  135  TEMP1(I,J)=ROWFQP(I)*COLFQP(J)
       TEMP2(I,J)=0.0
       GO TO 145
  140  TEMP1(I,J)=0.0
       TEMP2(I,J)=TABLE(I,J)
  145  TEMP3(I,J)=TEMP1(I,J)+TEMP2(I,J)
       WOT 6,230
       CALL WRITE1 (IDIM,JDIM,TEMP3)
       CALL GAMMA(IDIM,JDIM,TEMP3)
       CALL ASLAMB (IDIM,JDIM,TEMP3)
 2000  RETURN
       END

       SUBROUTINE GAMMA (IDIM,JDIM,TABLE)
C      THIS SUBROUTINE COMPUTES GAMMA
       DIMENSION TABLE(18,18),SUM1(18,18),SUM2(18,18)
 1000  FORMAT(12X,24HGAMMA FOR THIS TABLE IS F8.6,///)
       S=0.0
       D=0.0
       IDIM1=IDIM-1
       JDIM1=JDIM-1
       DO 5 I=1,IDIM
       DO 5 J=1,JDIM
       SUM1(I,J)=0.0
    5  SUM2(I,J)=0.0
       DO 10 I=1,IDIM1
       DO 10 J=1,JDIM1
       I1=I+1
       J1=J+1
       DO 15 II=I1,IDIM
       DO 15 JJ=J1,JDIM
   15  SUM1(I,J)=SUM1(I,J)+TABLE(II,JJ)
   10  S=S+SUM1(I,J)*TABLE(I,J)
       DO 20 I=1,IDIM1
       DO 20 J=2,JDIM
       I1=I+1
       JM1=J-1
       DO 25 II=I1,IDIM
       DO 25 JJ=1,JM1
   25  SUM2(I,J)=SUM2(I,J)+TABLE(II,JJ)
   20  D=D+SUM2(I,J)*TABLE(I,J)
       GAMMA=(S-D)/(S+D)
       WOT 6,1000,GAMMA
       RETURN
       END
```

153

```
      SUBROUTINE ASLAMB (IDIM,JDIM,TABLE)
C     THIS SUBROUTINE COMPUTES ASYMMETRIC LAMBDA, ROWS PRECEDE COLUMNS
      DIMENSION TABLE(18,18),COLTOT(18),ROWMAX(18)
 1000 FORMAT (12X,69HASYMMETRIC LAMBDA FOR THIS TABLE, ROWS LOGICALLY P
     1ECEDE COLUMNS, IS ,F8.6,///)
      TOTAL=0.0
      DO 10 J=1,JDIM
   10 COLTOT(J)=0.0
      DO 15 I=1,IDIM
      DO 15 J=1,JDIM
   15 COLTOT(J)=COLTOT(J)+TABLE(I,J)
      DO 20 J=1,JDIM
   20 TOTAL=TOTAL+COLTOT(J)
      CMARMX=COLTOT(1)
      DO 30 J=2,JDIM
      IF(CMARMX-COLTOT(J)) 25,30,30
   25 CMARMX=COLTOT(J)
   30 CONTINUE
      SUM=0.0
      DO 45 I=1,IDIM
      ROWMAX(I)=TABLE(I,1)
      DO 40 J=2,JDIM
      IF(ROWMAX(I)-TABLE(I,J)) 35,40,40
   35 ROWMAX(I)=TABLE(I,J)
   40 CONTINUE
   45 SUM=SUM+ROWMAX(I)
      DAMBDA=(SUM-SMARMX)/(TOTAL-SMARMX)
      WOT 6,1000,DAMBDA
      RETURN
      END

      SUBROUTINE WRITE1 (IDIM,JDIM,TABLE)
C  THIS SUBROUTINE WRITES A TABLE WITHOUT TOTALS
      DIMENSION TABLE(17,17),BLOCK(17,17),HOLD(17,17)
      DIMENSION NOCOL(17)
      COMMON NEW,HOLD,BLOCK
  100 FORMAT (2X,10HCOL NUMBER ,10(5X,I2,5X),/,12X,10(5X,I2,5X),//)
  110 FORMAT (2X,7HROW NO. ,I3,10F12.4,/,12X,10F12.4,//)
  130 FORMAT (/)
  140 FORMAT (//)
      DO 5 J=1,JDIM
    5 NOCOL(J)=J
      WOT 6,100,(NOCOL(J),J=1,JDIM )
      WOT 6,130
      DO 10  I=1,IDIM
      WOT 6, 110, I,(TABLE(I,J),J=1,JDIM)
   10 WOT 6,130
      WOT 6,140
      RETURN
      END

      SUBROUTINE WRITE2(IDIM,JDIM,T)
C  THIS SUBROUTINE WRITES A TABLE WITH TOTALS COMPUTED WITHIN SUBROUTINE
      DIMENSION ROW(17),COL(17),T(17,17),NOCOL(17)
 1000FORMAT ( 1X,
     1        10HROW TOTALS,12X,9(2X,7HCOL NO.,I3),/,24X,9(9X,I3),//)
  110 FORMAT (F11.4,2X,7HROW NO.,I3,9F12.4,/,23X,9F12.4)
  120 FORMAT(/,F11.4,2X,10HCOL TOTALS,9F12.4,/,23X,9F12.4,///)
  130 FORMAT (/)
      DO 15 I=1,IDIM
   15 ROW(I)=0.0
      DO 20 J=1,JDIM
   20 COL(J)=0.0
      DO 25 I=1,IDIM
      DO 25 J=1,JDIM
      ROW(I)=ROW(I)+T(I,J)
   25 COL(J)=COL(J)+T(I,J)
```

154

```
      TOTAL=0.0
      DO 32 I=1,IDIM
   32 TOTAL=TOTAL+ROW(I)
      DO 5 J=1,JDIM
    5 NOCOL(J)=J
      WOT 6,100,(NOCOL(J),J=1,JDIM)
      WOT 6,130
      DO 10 I=1,IDIM
      WOT 6,110,ROW(I),I,(T(I,J),J=1,JDIM)
   10 WOT 6,130
      WOT 6,120,TOTAL,(COL(J),J=1,JDIM)
      WOT 6,130
      RETURN
      END
```

Estimating the maximum index of dissimilarity

In this appendix we continue the discussion of Section 5.7. By considering arrays of increasing complexity we shall develop an algorithm for identifying the table "most-different" from a given table, in the sense of Section 5.7.

Case 1: A univariate distribution.

Suppose we were given only a set of frequencies $|n_i; i = 1, \ldots, r|$ with total frequency N. That is, we have a set of r frequencies with a constraint on the total frequency, N. The MDT for such an array is $|m_i; i = 1, \ldots, r|$ defined by

$$
m_i = \begin{cases} N \text{ for one value of } i = i' \text{ such that } n_{i'} = \min_i(n_i) \\ \\ 0 \text{ for all other } i. \end{cases}
$$

Then,

$$
D_{max} = \Sigma_i |n_i - m_i| = |n_{i'} - m_{i'}| + \Sigma_{i \neq i'} |n_i - m_i|
$$

$$
= (N - \min_i(n_i)) + (N - \min_i(n_i))
$$

and

$$
\Delta_{max} = 1 - (1/N)\min_i (n_i).
$$

The proof is trivial: if a frequency less than N is fitted to cell i', defined above, then D will be less than the D_{max} above, etc.

This case can be extended to a bivariate (or, even more gener-

ally, a multivariate) distribution with constraints only on, say, column totals. D_{max} for the entire array will be obtained when sums of absolute differences in each column are maximized individually. Let the array be $|m_{ij}; i = 1, \ldots, r$ and $j = 1, \ldots, c|$ with constraints on $\Sigma_j n_{ij} = n_i$ (and $\Sigma_i n_i = N$). The MDT $|m_{ij}|$ will be

$$
m_{ij} \quad = \quad
\begin{cases}
n_i \text{ for one cell } (i, j) = (i, j') \text{ in each row } i \\
\qquad\qquad \text{such that } n_{ij'} = \min_j n_{ij} \\
0 \text{ for all other } (i, j).
\end{cases}
$$

Then,

$$
D_{max} = \Sigma_i 2(n_i - \min_j (n_{ij}))
$$

and

$$
\Delta_{max} = 1 - (1/N) \Sigma_i \min_j (n_{ij}).
$$

If constraints on *both* row and column total were present, the additional constraints would necessarily reduce Δ_{max} relative to constraints on just rows or just columns. That is, if Δ_{max} is the maximum value of Δ in the bivariate case, and if

$$
\Delta_1 = 1 - (1/N) \Sigma_i \min_j (n_{ij})
$$

$$
\Delta_2 = 1 - (1/N) \Sigma_j \min_i (n_{ij})
$$

then $\max(\Delta_1, \Delta_2)$ gives an upper bound for Δ_{max}, Note, however, that one cannot assert that $\Delta_{max} \leqslant \min (\Delta_1, \Delta_2)$. The final observation for the univariate case is that the number of cells in the MDT that are assigned the value zero is equal to the number of degrees of freedom in the array under the constraints given.

Case 2: Two-way tables with one degree of freedom (i.e., 2 x 2 tables).

Let $T_0 = |n_{ij}|$ be a 2 x 2 table, with the MDT, $|m_{ij}|$, constrained to T_0 on both row and column totals. Let (i', j') be the cell such that

$$
n_{i'j'} = \max [\min (n_{11}, n_{22}), \min (n_{12}, n_{21})].
$$

157

Then it can be shown that

$$m_{ij} = \begin{cases} 0 \text{ for } (i', j') \\ \text{as implied by marginals for other } (i, j). \end{cases}$$

That is, we assign $m_{i'j'} = 0$ and, since we have only one degree of freedom in a 2×2 table, then fill in the MDT as implied. D_{max} and Δ_{max} follow, but their formulas do not simplify in this case nor in subsequent examples.

The proof proceeds in two steps.

It is understood that $|n_{ij}|$ and $|m_{ij}|$ are 2×2, non-negative, etc.

Theorem 1. At least one frequency in $|m_{ij}|$ will be zero.

Proof. We can re-write n_{ij} and m_{ij} as shown in Table A1, first and second panels, respectively (n_{11} is known, x is to be found). When the tables are written in this format, D becomes simply $D = \Sigma_{i,j} |n_{ij} - m_{ij}| = 4 |n_{11} - x|$. Now, since $|m_{ij}|$ is a table of frequencies, we have

$$x \geqslant 0$$

$$n_{1.} - x \geqslant 0, \text{ i.e., } x \leqslant n_{1.}$$

$$n_{.1} - x \geqslant 0, \text{ i.e., } x \leqslant n_{.1}$$

$$x + (n_{.2} - n_{1.}) \geqslant 0, \text{ i.e., } x \geqslant (n_{1.} - n_{.2}).$$

Summarizing, $\max (0, n_{1.} - n_{.2}) \leqslant x \leqslant \min (n_{1.}, n_{.1})$.

But D is a monotonic increasing function of x for $x \geqslant n_{11}$ and a monotonic decreasing function of x for $x \leqslant n_{11}$, i.e., D will assume its maximum either when x is a maximum *or* when x is a minimum, so that at least one of the following is true in the MDT:

(1) $x = 0$,	i.e., $m_{11} = 0$	
or (2) $x = n_1 - n_2$,	i.e., $m_{22} = 0$	
or (3) $x = n_{1.}$	i.e., $m_{12} = 0$	
or (4) $x = n_{.1}$	i.e., $m_{21} = 0$.	Q.E.D.

Corollary

The cell which, when set to zero, will maximize D, is that in which $\max [\min (n_{11}, n_{22}), \min (n_{12}, n_{21})]$ is located.

TABLE A1.

The known T_0 and its MDT written in terms of their single degree of freedom.

n_{11}	$n_{1.} - n_{11}$	$n_{1.}$	x	$n_{1.} - x$	$n_{1.}$
$n_{.1} - n_{11}$	$n_{11} + (n_{.2} - n_{1.})$	$n_{2.}$	$n_{.1} - x$	$x + (n_{.2} - n_{1.})$	$n_{2.}$
$n_{.1}$	$n_{.2}$	N	$n_{.1}$	$n_{.2}$	N

Proof. Given the results in the proof of Theorem 1, this rule can be proved by simple manipulation. In practice, we only require Theorem 1. We can compute D for all possible choices of the "zero-cell", selecting D_{max} from this set of D's.

Case 3: One degree of freedom in a larger table.

When interior cells are constrained, a single degree of freedom *may* arise on a table of any size with an even number of unblocked cells. The simplest case with more than four unblocked cells is shown in Figure A1, in which a cell with an X is constrained.

Theorem 1 generalizes directly to this larger table, since $D = 6 |n_{12} - x|$ for appropriate x. The least upper bound of x is determined by cells n_{13}, n_{21}, and n_{32} ; the greatest lower bound of x is determined by cells n_{12}, n_{23}, and n_{31} in this illustration. A useful algorithm for locating the cell (i, j) which, when set to 0, will yield the MDT and D_{max} is as follows: (i, j) is the cell where max [min (n_{13}, n_{21}, n_{32}), min (n_{12}, n_{23}, n_{31})] is located. When a computer is available, however, all cases of a single degree of freedom are handled by trial-and-error location of the correct "zero-cell."

X		
	X	
		X

Fig. A1. One degree
of freedom with six
unblocked cells.

Case 4: Multiple single degrees of freedom.

It may well happen that we have more than one degree of freedom but the degrees of freedom are separable into single degrees of freedom. That is, by fixing any particular frequency, we automatically (via the marginals) fix a total of an even number of cells (including the first one). The two simplest cases of two separable degrees of freedom are shown in Figure A2. At first sight the left panel has $4 + 4 - 1 = 7$ constraints and 8 free cells. But it does *not* have $8 - 7 = 1$ degree of freedom, since the free cells are arranged in two separate blocs. We can maximize each bloc separately through the correct selection of two zero-cells, one in each of the two blocs. The right panel has $4 + 3 - 1 = 6$ constraints and 8 free cells. It has $8 - 6 = 2$ degrees of freedom and the two are separable. If we fix any one of the four cells in the upper right portion, we fix them all. Similarly for the lower left portion. Separability is also discussed by Goodman (1968a) and Mantel (1970).

Given the variation in patterns of free cells which produce exactly one degree of freedom, exceedingly complex patterns can be reducible to multiple single degrees of freedom in which D_{max} can be computed exactly by successively maximizing over each single degree of freedom.

The general rule for identifying a case of multiple single degrees of freedom is this: that as *any* specific free cell is fitted, an odd number of other free cells are uniquely determined by the fitted frequency and the table marginals.

Computational procedure

A brief discussion of the computational routine used may help clarify the separation of the single degrees of freedom in this case.

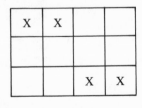

Fig. A2. Two separable degrees of freedom: the two simplest basic patterns.

An array called PARITY is formed for each single degree of freedom *in turn,* under this definition:

$$\text{PARITY } (i, j) = \begin{cases} 0 \text{ for an unaffected cell} \\ -1 \text{ or } 1 \text{ for an affected cell} \end{cases}$$

with the constraint that PARITY adds to zero in each row and in each column. (The term "parity" is employed somewhat arbitrarily in the sense of "equal vs. not equal" to divide affected cells into two classes, those of "positive parity" and those of "negative parity".) Table A2 gives the successive PARITY arrays for the right panel of Figure A2.

The choice of which non-zero cells in PARITY will be positive and which will be negative is arbitrary (though subject to the constraint). The signs indicate that in a fitted table, if we add a frequency δ to any *positive*-parity cell, then we must add δ to *all* such cells and must subtract δ from all *negative*-parity cells (or vice versa) in order to maintain marginals. Using this notation, it is easy to fix a cell frequency and cycle through the PARITY array, filling in the whole table. It should be noted that when some cell frequencies are fixed (at zero, say), certain implied frequencies will be negative. As soon as a negative cell frequency is computed, the "fitting" which led to it is discarded.

The PARITY arrays themselves are obtained as follows. Under the general rule for identifying a case of multiple single degrees of freedom, there may be some rows or columns with more than two free cells. We first locate any *rows* with more than two free cells, then (a) set PARITY $(i, j) = + 1$ in the first free cell in that row, then (b) locate the (only) other free cell in the same column, and set PARITY $(i, j) = -1$ for that cell. (There can be but one other free cell in the same column, since if there were two, say, neither

TABLE A2.

PARITY arrays for the right panel of Figure A2.

0	0	0	0
1	−1	0	0
−1	1	0	0

0	0	1	−1
0	0	−1	1
0	0	0	0

frequency would be determined exactly.) We then (c) locate the (only) other free cell in the same row we began with, in (a). After fitting the cells above, so they are no longer free cells, we repeat the procedure for any other rows with more than two free cells.

PARITY is obtained in a similar way, afterwards, for all remaining patterns of free cells, whether there are any *columns* left with more than two free cells or not. We locate the first free cell in a column with more than two free cells (or the first cell in the whole table, lexicographically) and for that cell put PARITY $(i, j) = +1$. We then reverse the order of (b) and (c) above, cycling through steps (c) and (b) until led back to a free cell in the same row we began with in (a).

For tables of the preceding type we have given a proof that D_{max} and Δ_{max} can be computed and algorithms for finding the MDT, D_{max} and Δ_{max}. We now offer algorithms for the more general case, but cannot provide a proof to accompany them.

Case 5: The general r x c table with some cells blocked.

If we are given a table with f degrees of freedom, then we can apply this theorem:

Theorem 2. The MDT will be a table in which at least f linearly independent, unblocked cells are assigned zero frequency.

Proof. The proof is a generalization of that of Theorem 1. We can select a set of f linearly independent cells of T_0 and express the remaining cells as linear combinations of them. Then we can express the MDT in the same way, with the same choice of fundamental set. D is then expressed as a sum of absolute differences in which the only variables are f frequencies in the MDT, as yet unknown. D will be bi-monotonic in each of these f frequencies; that is, when all of the $f - 1$ other frequencies are held constant, D will increase as the remaining one increases above a certain value or as it decreases below this value. Consequently, D will achieve a local maximum for each configuration of the f frequencies at their respective lower or upper bounds. As in the case of $f = 1$, each such configuration will involve setting one frequency of the table equal to zero for each degree of freedom (it may happen that additional cells will be set to zero by implication of the marginals only).

To summarize, as each of the F fundamental sets is put entirely to zero, we obtain a local maximum of D, in the sense that D will be reduced if any one of the cells in the set is assigned a small positive frequency.

162

A detailed proof would be by induction on f.

Q.E.D.

According to Theorem 2, an exact solution for the MDT could be found by cycling over all fundamental sets, in turn setting their total frequencies in T_0 to zero, filling in the remaining cells, computing D, and selecting that table which generates the largest D as the MDT. In practice, however, too many fundamental sets exist for such a cycling procedure to be practicable, even with a computer. We can verify the impracticability by computing F, the number of fundamental sets, in a r x c table with no interior constraints and a full $(r - 1)(c - 1)$ degrees of freedom. This amounts to computing the number of combinations of $(r - 1)$ $(c - 1)$ cells taken out of rc cells such that (1) there are no rows with all c cells taken out, (2) there are no columns with all r cells taken out.

The number of ways of taking $(r - 1)(c - 1)$ cells out of rc, without restrictions, is simply

$$F_1 = \binom{rc}{(r - 1)(c - 1)}$$

The number of these patterns which have one or more complete rows removed, and violate (1) above, is

$$F_2 = r \binom{rc - c}{(r - 1)(c - 1) - c}$$

F_2 is obtained by counting the number of combinations in which a row is completely removed (c cells in one row are removed) and noting that there are r ways of selecting this row.

Similarly, the number of patterns of the first F_1 which have one or more complete columns removed is

$$F_3 = c \binom{rc - r}{(r - 1)(c - 1) - r}$$

Some combinations are duplicated in the last two totals. The number of combinations with at least one full row *and* at least one full column removed is

163

$$F_4 = rc \left(\begin{array}{c} rc - r - c + 1 \\ (r - 1)\ (c - 1)\ - r - c + 1 \end{array} \right)$$

Thus $F = F_1 - F_2 - F_3 + F_4$ is the number of fundamental sets. In the case of a square table, with $c = r$, we have

$$F = \left(\begin{array}{c} r^2 \\ (r - 1)^2 \end{array} \right) - 2r \left(\begin{array}{c} r(r - 1) \\ (r - 1)^2 - r \end{array} \right) + r^2 \left(\begin{array}{c} (r - 1)^2 \\ (r - 1)^2 - 2r + 1 \end{array} \right)$$

If $r = 3$, then $F = 90$. For $r = 5$, $F = 375,000$. For $r = 9$ or $r = 17$, which we shall consider later, F is astronomical. It is necessary to find a procedure that will yield the "zero fundamental set" with the largest D and Δ, or that will approximate this set.

Sequential estimation

If we are to find which fundamental set should be put to zero without listing all fundamental sets and computing D for each of them, we must select a strategy for fixing cells in the MDT in some sequence. We must have rules for (1) which cell(s) to fix at each step of the sequence, and for (2) what values to assign to these cells. Based on the preceding discussion, it should be clear that if we are going to assign a value to a free cell it should be either (a) the least we can put in that cell, or (b) the most we can put in that cell, viz. the minimum of (i) the frequency yet to be assigned to the given row and (ii) the frequency yet to be assigned to the given column.

The difficulty is in selecting the sequence in which cells will be assigned in our estimate of the MDT. There are two aspects of this difficulty. The first is the selection of a good stepwise maximization criterion. The second is guarding against "impossible inner tables" (which we can refer to as IIT). The IIT will be discussed first.

Impossible inner tables

For any T_0 whatever, a substantial number of the F fundamental sets *cannot* be set to zero without implying negative frequencies in some of the remaining cells as the table is filled in. In fact, after assigning very few cells (either as zero or as their "maximum possible") under certain marginal distributions (particularly under highly non-uniform distributions), there is *no* way one can assign the remaining degrees of freedom and conclude with a table of non-negative frequencies. It then becomes necessary to backtrack and to assign cells in some different sequence.

An example is furnished in Table A3. The left panel is T_0. The right panel is a stage in the estimation of the MDT at which cell $(3, 3)$ has been assigned the value 0 (and has, in effect, been constrained or blocked out, so is given an X). (Note that when we constrain cells for the model of quasi-independence, we in effect set them to zero and subtract their fixed frequency from the marginals, so that an IIT cannot arise. In the present case we are trying to construct a table with the same marginals as T_0 but with some frequencies set at zero, so that when a cell is set at zero the marginals are unchanged.)

Let $|n_i. ; i = 1, \ldots, r|$ and $|n._j; j = 1, \ldots, c|$ be the row and column marginals, as before, and use the array $|b_{ij}|$ to describe which cells have been set to zero or blocked or constrained in any way. That is,

$$b_{ij} = \begin{cases} 1 \text{ if } (i, j) \text{ is a free cell} \\ 0 \text{ if } (i, j) \text{ has been fitted, etc.} \end{cases}$$

Then we will have an IIT if there exists any row i such that $n_i.> \Sigma_j b_{ij} n._j$ or if there exists any column j such that $n._j > \Sigma_i b_{ij} n_i.$. The right panel of Table A3 is an IIT because $8 = n_3. = n._3 > 3 + 3 = 6$. In words, we require 8 cases for row (and column) three but only 6 cases are available, since we cannot put any cases in cell $(3, 3)$.

An impossible inner table can arise in other ways, although the above condition is a symptom of most cases I have computed. An IIT may pass the above test, but fail the following generalization.

TABLE A3.

T_0 and the marginals of T_0 with cell $(3,3)$ constrained to zero.

1	1	1	3
1	1	1	3
1	1	6	8
3	3	8	14

			3
			3
		X	8
3	3	8	14

We can pool all rows with the same pattern of free cells, adding their required row frequencies, and pool all columns with the same pattern of free cells, adding their required row frequencies. If the above check is applied to this "condensed" table we may find that more cases are required for a *bloc* of cells than can possibly be packed into that bloc, even though for the original table, the "available vs. required" frequency test was passed.

However, there are other types of IIT not so easily diagnosed, and some general criterion, based only on $|n_{i.}|$, $|n_{.j}|$, and $|b_{ij}|$ is required if the sequential estimation of the MDT is not to break down.

The simple test given above is applied to the uncondensed table alone, and inner tables which pass it are given the following, definitive test. The model of quasi-independence uses only the above three arrays to estimate interior expected frequencies. Under the assumption that it is *possible* to fill in a table with positive frequencies, the standard iterative procedures for obtaining quasi-independent expectations are generally believed to converge (according to Wagner (1970), convergence has not yet been proved). With an IIT, however, we cannot fill in the table at all without using some negative frequencies. In particular, if the table is filled in such that each frequency is the product of row and column factors, then some of these quasi-independent (as it were) estimates will be negative and some row and/or column factors will be negative.

Table A4 provides an example. The left panel shows the required marginals, with cell (3, 3) held out. The right panel gives a table which meets all these constraints, with entries which are products of row and column effects, also shown (with the first row factor anchored at unity).

TABLE A4.

One IIT and the "quasi-independent" table it generates.

			1		$-1/4$	$-1/4$	$3/2$	1 (1)
			1		$-1/4$	$-1/4$	$3/2$	1 (1)
		X	3		$3/2$	$3/2$	X	3 (-6)
1	1	3	5		1	1	3	5
					$(-1/4)$	$(-1/4)$	$(3/2)$	

166

The usual computing procedures for quasi-independent estimates are unable to give the "solution" in Table A4 (an algebraic version was used for this example) or in any IIT because (assuming positive quantities are used to start the iterative process) only positive row and column factors can be produced. The usual procedures, when adapted to such a situation, will rapidly *diverge*, with some estimates of factors becoming smaller and some becoming larger with each iteration. Thus, divergence of the procedure is the conclusive indication of an IIT. The computer program of Appendix 1 checks first for the simpler type of IIT described on the previous page for reasons of efficiency (the simpler type seems to be most common and is easy to check for), but the divergence test could be used for all types.

It is paradoxical that in the effort to evaluate the model of quasi-independence, we should be led to use of the convergence property of the model to help compute an evaluative measure. It should be clear that this use does not contaminate the measure, since the model's only role at this stage is to establish an existence condition, and not to estimate quantities which will be used in any other way.

The basic logic of the preceding few pages is that

(1) using some criterion (to be discussed next) we fill in or fit a cell in the MDT, the table with the same marginals as T_0 which is "most different" from T_0;

(2) as each cell is fitted, we automatically fill in any cells which may be precisely implied by the marginals and cells fitted thus far;

(3) the cells not thus far filled form an "inner table" of T_0 which is subject to revised marginal constraints;

(4) if the inner table cannot possibly be filled in with positive numbers, we return to (1) above, revising the choice of cell to be fitted;

(5) if the inner table *can* be filled in with positive numbers, we check whether it consists of multiple single degrees of freedom, in which case we can easily maximize the sum of absolute differences in the inner table;

(6) if degrees of freedom remain which are not multiple single d.f., then we return to (1) and use the criterion to fit an additional cell of the MDT, etc.

The procedure described above is guaranteed to generate a table with as many cells fitted to zero as there are degrees of freedom in T_0 (as a minimum). Thus the table generated is, by Theorem 2, a candidate for the MDT. The quality of the estimated MDT will depend mainly on the quality of the criterion in step (1).

The reason why we can obtain a candidate for the MDT, regardless of the criterion employed, is as follows, and is rather simple. At each step of the fitting operation we check to make sure we have a table that can be filled in with positive entries. However, it is not difficult to prove that every such table, with a compatible set of marginals and constraints, can be filled in with (at least) as many cells fitted to zero as there are degrees of freedom in that table; this holds, in particular, for what we have called "inner" tables. Thus we can sequentially identify a fundamental set which can be entirely fitted to zero.

The fitting criterion

Two minimax criteria were used independently. In the great majority of cases in which both were tried, they gave the same results. In remaining cases, either one might yield a slightly higher value than the other. The second criterion given was used more often and is perhaps somewhat preferable, for reasons to be given.

The cell chosen to be fitted was that which maximized the minimum sum of absolute differences over the inner table (all cells not yet fitted) at the given stage of estimation. Specifically:

I. Packing cells

Suppose we fit to cell (i, j) the maximum number of cases that cell can hold, i.e., the minimum of (a) the remaining sum to be fitted to row i, and (b) the remaining sum to be fitted to column j. This type of fit is suggested by the univariate case, for example. Depending on whether (a) or (b) is a minimum, the unfitted cells in row i or column j will be set to zero, except for the packed cell (i, j). That is, we actually fit a whole row or column at the same time.

It is easy to compute the minimum contribution to D which will result from packing cell (i, j), from row i, from column j, and from the remaining unfitted cells. Rather than developing notation and stating the contribution here, we refer to the program in the appendix to this chapter. At each stage we first try to pack the cell for which the minimum contribution is largest. If we are led to an IIT by the choice, we try packing the next "most promising" cell, etc.

II. Setting cells to zero

With this criterion cells are fitted to zero. The minimum

168

contribution to D which results from setting cell (i, j) to zero can again be separated into components from cell (i, j), from row i, from column j, and from the remainder of the table. The cell for which this minimum contribution is greatest is set to zero first, checked, etc. The separate contributions can, again, be found in the program in Appendix 7.

I have a slight preference for this procedure because it responds more directly to Theorem 2, in that we are, basically, searching for a fundamental set which can be put entirely to zero.

Revising the estimate

Once we have, through the above procedures, obtained a candidate for the MDT, it is worthwhile checking whether a relatively slight change would produce another table with a fundamental set fitted to zero but with a larger value of D and Δ.

Say that two fundamental sets of f cells are *adjacent* if they have $f - 1$ cells in common. The estimated MDT was revised by cycling over fundamental sets adjacent to the one generated above by, in effect, transferring each zero-cell to all possible other locations in the table and checking for a possibly larger value of D. If a better set was found, then it was cycled over, etc. In practice, as many as ten revisions to the initial estimate were rare, although the program allowed for a great many (approximately 20f).

There is still no assurance that by moving through a sequence of adjacent fundamental sets we can eventually reach the true MDT. All fundamental sets can, of course, be arranged by an adjacent sequencing, in many ways, and it is possible to get from a computed fundamental set to that of the true MDT by several series of adjacencies. *However,* since we are dealing with sets of zero frequencies, many sets in any sequence are likely to imply tables with negative frequencies, and to disrupt the sequence's availability through the "revision" process. Second, any sequence would be likely to have its own local maxima and minima of D and Δ. At best, the revision procedure permits us to obtain a local maximum in a sequence of adjacent patterns leading to the MDT. Yet there are indications that the estimate of Δ_{max} is quite accurate.

APPENDIX 7

Program listing for computation of the maximum index of dissimilarity

The following Fortran II computer program computes the value of Δ_{max} for a given input table and blocking. The only definitions necessary for use of the program are given in Appendix 5. Formatting is the same for this program and for the one in Appendix 5, and is explicit in both main programs. A code symbol, INDEX, which must follow each blocking read into the machine, is defined at the end of the following main program.

```
C       THIS PROGRAM COMPUTES THE MAXIMUM POSSIBLE COEFFICIENT OF
C       DISSIMILARITY BETWEEN A THEORETICAL TABLE AND A GIVEN TABLE
C       USING A PROCEDURE WHICH LOCATES CELLS WITH MAXIMIN
C       CONTRIBUTIONS TO THE INDEX OF DISSIMILARITY
        DIMENSION TABLE(17,17),BLOCK(17,17),BTEMP(17,17),TEMP1(17,17)
        DIMENSION TEMP2(17,17),ROWTOT(17),COLTOT(17),BRTOT(17),BCTOT(17)
        DIMENSION TMAX(17,17),THOLD(17,17),BHOLD(17,17),TDIFS(17,17)
        DIMENSION SUMROW(17),SUMCOL(17)
        DIMENSION PLUG(17,17)
        DIMENSION ABLE(17,17)
        DIMENSION HOLD(17,17)
        COMMON TABLE,BLOCK,BTEMP,TEMP1,TEMP2,ROWTOT,COLTOT,BRTOT,BCTOT,
       1BTOT,IDIM,JDIM,KEY,NEW,HOLD
 1000 FORMAT(1H1,10X,15HINPUT TABLE NO. ,I3, 18H WITH BLOCKING NO. ,
       1I3,//)
 4000 FORMAT(10X,5HKEY=   ,I2)
 5000 FORMAT (3I2)
 5100 FORMAT (8F10.4)
 5010 FORMAT (80F1.0)
 5200 FORMAT (I1)
C       PART I   READ INPUT
    2 RIT 5,5000,NAME,IDIM,JDIM
      RIT 5,5100, ((TABLE(I,J),J=1,JDIM),I=1,IDIM)
    1 RIT 5,5000,NBLOCK,NEW,NEW
      IDIM=NEW
      JDIM=NEW
      NA=IDIM*JDIM
      RIT 5,5010, ((BLOCK(I,J), J=1,JDIM), I=1,IDIM)
C       PART II  OBTAIN FIRST COMPLETE ESTIMATE OF THE MOST DIFFERENT
C       TABLE
C        INITIALIZATION
      KKEY=2
```

```
      DO 5 I=1,IDIM
      DO 5 J=1,JDIM
      PLUG(I,J)=BLOCK(I,J)
      THOLD(I,J)=TABLE(I,J)*BLOCK(I,J)
      TMAX(I,J)=0.0
    5 BHOLD(I,J)=BLOCK(I,J)
    6 WOT 6,1000,NAME,NBLOCK
      CALL WRITE2(IDIM,JDIM,THOLD)
      KERR7=0
    7 TOPLIM=1000000.0
      KERR8=0
    8 DO 9 I=1,IDIM
      DO 9 J=1,JDIM
      TEMP1(I,J)=THOLD(I,J)
      TEMP2(I,J)=TMAX(I,J)
    9 BTEMP(I,J)=BHOLD(I,J)
      DO 10 I=1,IDIM
      BRTOT(I)=0.0
      SUMROW(I)=0.0
   10 ROWTOT(I)=0.0
      DO 15 J=1,JDIM
      BCTOT(J)=0.0
      SUMCOL(J)=0.0
   15 COLTOT(J)=0.0
      BTOT=0.0
      DO 17 I=1,IDIM
      DO 17 J=1,JDIM
C     TOTALS YET TO BE ALLOCATED
      ROWTOT(I)=ROWTOT(I)+TABLE(I,J)*BLOCK(I,J)-TMAX(I,J)
      COLTOT(J)=COLTOT(J)+TABLE(I,J)*BLOCK(I,J)-TMAX(I,J)
C     FIXED TOTALS OVER CELLS NOT YET FITTED
      SUMROW(I)=SUMROW(I)+TEMP1(I,J)
C     RECOMPUTE TDIFS ONLY IF LAST CELL PACKED DID NOT YIELD AN
C     INCONSISTENCY
   17 SUMCOL(J)=SUMCOL(J)+TEMP1(I,J)
      GO TO (405,20),KKEY
C      FIND THE CELL WITH THE GREATEST MAXIMINCONTRIBUTION TO INDEX
   20 DO 40 I=1,IDIM
      DO 40 J=1,JDIM
      TDIFS(I,J)=0.0
      IF(BTEMP(I,J)) 40,40,205
  205 IF( PLUG(I,J)) 40,40,21
   21 A=0.0
      B=0.0
      T=TEMP1(I,J)
      DO 30 II=1,IDIM
      DO 30 JJ=1,JDIM
      IF(II-I)  25,30,25
   25 A=A+ROWTOT(II)
      IF(JJ-J) 27,30,27
   27 B=B+BTEMP(II,JJ)*TEMP1(II,JJ)
   30 CONTINUE
      TDIFS(I,J)= T+ABSF(ROWTOT(I)-SUMROW(I)+T) +ABSF(COLTOT(J)-
     1SUMCOL(J)+T) +ABSF(A-COLTOT(J)-B)
   40 CONTINUE
  405 BOTTOM=0.0
      DO 44 I=1,IDIM
      DO 44 J=1,JDIM
      IF(BTEMP(I,J)) 44,44,407
  407 IF( PLUG(I,J)) 44,44,41
   41 IF(TDIFS(I,J)-TOPLIM) 42,44,44
   42 IF(TDIFS(I,J)-BOTTOM) 44,44,43
   43 II=I
      JJ=J
      BOTTOM=TDIFS(I,J)
   44 CONTINUE
      BTEMP(II,JJ)=0.0
```

171

```
          TEMP2(II,JJ)=0.0
C         CELL(II,JJ) NEED NOT BE TRIED AGAIN, EITHER IT WILL BE SET TO
C         ZERO OR IT CANNOT BE SET TO ZERO
          PLUG(II,JJ)=0.0
       75 DO 80 I=1,IDIM
          DO 80 J=1,JDIM
          BRTOT(I)=BRTOT(I)+BTEMP(I,J)
          BCTOT(J)=BCTOT(J)+BTEMP(I,J)
       80 BTOT=BTOT+BTEMP(I,J)
          NB=XFIXF(BTOT)+5
          KEY=1
          CALL FILL(TEMP2,ROWTOT,COLTOT,BTEMP,BRTOT,BCTOT,BTOT,IDIM,JDIM,
         1KEY)
C         THE KEY HERE IS AN OUTPUT OF SUBROUTINE FILL
C         FOR MEANING OF KEY SEE SUBROUTINE FILL
          GO TO (300,165,162,198), KEY
      300 TOPLIM=BOTTOM+1.0
          KKEY=1
          KERR8=KERR8+1
          IF(KERR8-NB)      8,8,230
      198 DO 199 I=1,IDIM
          DO 199 J=1,JDIM
          THOLD(I,J)=TEMP1(I,J)*BTEMP(I,J)
          BHOLD(I,J)=BTEMP(I,J)
      199 TMAX(I,J)=TEMP2(I,J)
C         IF NO MORE CONSTRAINED CELLS, THEN LOOK FOR ANOTHER CELL TO PACK
          KKEY=2
          KERR7=KERR7+1
          IF(KERR7-NA) 7,7,230
      162 CALL SINDF(TABLE,TEMP2,ROWTOT,COLTOT,BTEMP,BRTOT,BCTOT,BTOT,
         1IDIM,JDIM)
C         PART III   REFINE THE ESTIMATE OF THE MOST DIFFERENT TABLE
      165 CALL ADJPAT(TABLE,BLOCK,TEMP2,IDIM,JDIM)
      230 RIT 5,5200,INDEX
C         INDEX=1 MEANS SAME TABLE, NEW BLOCKING, INDEX=2 MEANS NEW TABLE
C         INDEX=3 MEANS CALL EXIT
          GO TO (1,2,3  ),INDEX
        3 CALL EXIT
          END

          SUBROUTINE ADJPAT(TABLE,BLOCK,TEMP2,IDIM,JDIM)
C         GIVEN A PATTERN OF ZERO-CELLS, THIS SUBROUTINE LOCATES AN
C         ADJACENT PATTERN(DIFFERING BY ONLY ONE ZERO-CELL) WITH A LARGER
C         INDEX OF DISSIMILARITY
          COMMON TABLE,BLOCK,BTEMP,TEMP1,TEMP2,ROWTOT,COLTOT,BRTOT,BCTOT,
         1BTOT,IDIM,JDIM,KEY,NEW,HOLD
          DIMENSION TABLE(17,17),BLOCK(17,17),BTEMP(17,17),TEMP1(17,17)
          DIMENSION TEMP2(17,17),ROWTOT(17),COLTOT(17),BRTOT(17),BCTOT(17)
          DIMENSION HOLD(17,17)
     1000 FORMAT (    30X,2HL=,I3,10X,3HLL=,I3   )
     2000 FORMAT(///,10X,62HTHE FOLLOWING IS THE TABLE MOST DIFFERENT FROM
         1HE INPUT TABLE, //)
          CALL COMP(TABLE,BLOCK,TEMP2,IDIM,JDIM)
          DO 15 I=1,IDIM
          DO 15 J=1,JDIM
          BTEMP(I,J)=TEMP2(I,J)
       15 TEMP1(I,J)=TABLE(I,J)*BLOCK(I,J)
          BTEMP(1,1)=1.0
          L=0
       32 L=L+1
          LL=0
C         SUCCESSIVELY RELEASE SINGLE ZERO CELLS AND SEARCH FOR BETTER ONES
          DO 70 I=1,IDIM
          DO 70 J=1,JDIM
          IF(BTEMP(I,J)) 35,35,70
       35 IF(BLOCK(I,J)) 70,70,40
       40 DO 67 II=1,IDIM
```

172

```
       DO 67 JJ=1,JDIM
       BTEMP(II,JJ)=1.0
       IF(TEMP2(II,JJ)) 66,66,67
   66  BTEMP(II,JJ)=0.0
   67  TEMP2(II,JJ)=0.0
       BTEMP(I,J)=1.0
C      MUST COMPUTE TOTALS
       BTOT=0.0
       DO 25 II=1,IDIM
       ROWTOT(II)=0.0
   25  BRTOT(II)=0.0
       DO 30 JJ=1,JDIM
       COLTOT(JJ)=0.0
   30  BCTOT(JJ)=0.0
       DO 33 II=1,IDIM
       DO 33 JJ=1,JDIM
       ROWTOT(II)=ROWTOT(II)+TEMP1(II,JJ)
       COLTOT(JJ)=COLTOT(JJ)+TEMP1(II,JJ)
       BRTOT(II)=BRTOT(II)+BTEMP(II,JJ)
       BCTOT(JJ)=BCTOT(JJ)+BTEMP(II,JJ)
   33  BTOT=BTOT+BTEMP(II,JJ)
       KEY=2
       CALL FILL(TEMP2,ROWTOT,COLTOT,BTEMP,BRTOT,BCTOT,PTOT,IDIM,JDIM,
      1KEY)
C      FOR MEANING OF KEY SEE SUBROUTINE FILL
       GO TO (80,70,150,150),KEY
  150  CALL SINDF(TABLE,TEMP2,ROWTOT,COLTOT,BTEMP,BRTOT,BCTOT,BTOT,
      1IDIM,JDIM)
C      IF SINDF GIVES US BACK THE PATTERN WE HAD BEFORE, THEN
C      TEMP2(I,J) WILL NOW BE ZERO AGAIN
       IF(TEMP2(I,J))70,70,55
   55  LL=LL+1
C      LL IS NUMBER OF CHANGES MADE WITHIN LATEST CYCLE THROUGH TABLE
C      L IS NUMBER OF CYCLES MADE THROUGH TABLE
       WOT 6,1000,L,LL
   70  CONTINUE
       IF(LL) 200,200,75
C      CYCLE THROUGH THE TABLE A MAXIMUM OF TWENTY TIMES
   75  IF(L-20) 32,32,200
   80  WOT 6,1500,KEY
 1500  FORMAT (10X,12HERROR, KEY= ,I2)
  200  WOT 6,2000
       CALL COMP(TABLE,BLOCK,TEMP2,IDIM,JDIM)
       CALL WRITE2(IDIM,JDIM,TEMP2)
       RETURN
       END

       SUBROUTINE FILL(TEMP2,ROWTOT,COLTOT,BTEMP,BRTOT,BCTOT,PTOT,
      1IDIM,JDIM,KEY)
C      THIS SUBROUTINE FILLS IN A TABLE AS MUCH AS POSSIBLE AS CERTAIN
C      CELLS BECOME FIXED
       COMMON TABLE,BLOCK,BTEMP,TEMP1,TEMP2,ROWTOT,COLTOT,BRTOT,BCTOT,
      1BTOT,IDIM,JDIM,KEY,NEW,HOLD
       DIMENSION TABLE(17,17),BLOCK(17,17),BTEMP(17,17),TEMP1(17,17)
       DIMENSION TEMP2(17,17),ROWTOT(17),COLTOT(17),BRTOT(17),BCTOT(17)
       DIMENSION R(17),C(17),HROW(17),HCOL(17)
       DIMENSION HOLD(17,17)
    1  M=0
       J=JDIM
       DO 25 I=1,IDIM
       IF(BRTOT(I)-1.0) 25,5,25
    5  DO 25 J=1,JDIM
       IF(BTEMP(I,J)) 25,25,10
   10  BTEMP(I,J)=0.0
       BRTOT(I)=BRTOT(I)-1.0
       BCTOT(J)=BCTOT(J)-1.0
       BTOT=BTOT-1.0
```

173

```
         TEMP2(I,J)=ROWTOT(I)
         COLTOT(J)=COLTOT(J)-ROWTOT(I)
         ROWTOT(I)=0.0
         IF(COLTOT(J)) 300,15,15
   15 IF(BTOT) 100,100,20
   20 M=M+1
   25 R(I)=0.0
         DO 50 J=1,JDIM
         IF(BCTOT(J)-1.0) 50,27,50
   27 DO 50 I=1,IDIM
         IF(BTEMP(I,J)) 50,50,30
   30 BTEMP(I,J)=0.0
         BRTOT(I)=BRTOT(I)-1.0
         BCTOT(J)=BCTOT(J)-1.0
         BTOT=BTOT-1.0
         TEMP2(I,J)=COLTOT(J)
         ROWTOT(I)=ROWTOT(I)-COLTOT(J)
         COLTOT(J)=0.0
         IF(ROWTOT(I)) 300,35,35
   35 IF(BTOT) 100,100,40
   40 M=M+1
   50 C(J)=0.0
         IF(M) 1,55,1
C        CHECK WHETHER POTENTIAL PATHOLOGICAL CASE
   55 GO TO (60,150), KEY
   60 DO 65 I=1,IDIM
         DO 65 J=1,JDIM
         R(I)=R(I)+COLTOT(J)*BTEMP(I,J)
   65 C(J)=C(J)+ROWTOT(I)*BTEMP(I,J)
         DO 70 I=1,IDIM
         IF(ROWTOT(I)-R(I)) 70,70,300
   70 CONTINUE
         DO 80 J=1,JDIM
         IF(COLTOT(J)-C(J)) 80,80,300
   80 CONTINUE
C        SET COLUMN FACTORS
         DO 410 J=1,JDIM
  410 C(J)=0.0
C        SET ROW FACTORS
         DO 420 I=1,IDIM
         R(I)=0.0
         IF(BRTOT(I)) 420,420,415
  415 R(I)=SQRTF(ROWTOT(I))
  420 CONTINUE
C        ANCHOR FIRST NON-ZERO ROW FACTOR
         DO 425 I=1,IDIM
         IF(BRTOT(I)) 425,425,430
  425 CONTINUE
  430 IT=I+1
C        ITERATION BEGINS
         KT=0
  435 KT=KT+1
         CLUE=0.0
         DO 455 J=1,JDIM
         HCOL(J)=0.0
         IF(BCTOT(J)) 455,455,440
  440 DO 450 I=1,IDIM
  450 HCOL(J)=HCOL(J)+BTEMP(I,J)*R(I)
         CJ  =COLTOT(J)/HCOL(J)
         ERR=ABSF(C(J)/CJ-1.0)
         IF(ERR-CLUE) 453,453,452
  452 CLUE=ERR
  453 C(J)=CJ
  455 CONTINUE
         DO 480 I=IT,IDIM
         HROW(I)=0.0
         IF(BRTOT(I)) 480,480,460
```

174

```
      460 DO 470 J=1,JDIM
      470 HROW(I)=HROW(I)+BTEMP(I,J)*C(J)
          RI   =ROWTOT(I)/HROW(I)
          ERR=ABSF(R(I)/RI-1.0)
          IF(ERR-CLUE) 476,476,474
      474 CLUE=ERR
      476 R(I)=RI
      480 CONTINUE
C         ASSUME CONVERGENCE AS SOON AS MAXIMUM RELATIVE CHANGE BETWEEN
C         ITERATIONS IS FIVE PERCENT OR LESS
          IF(CLUE-.05) 150,150,490
C         ASSUME NO CONVERGENCE AFTER FORTY ITERATIONS
      490 IF(KT-40) 435,485,485
      485 CONTINUE
      300 KEY=1
C         KEY=1 MEANS THE GIVEN FIXED CELLS ARE INCOMPATIBLE WITH MARGINALS
          GO TO 200
      100 KEY=2
C         KEY=2 MEANS ALL CELLS ARE FILLED
          GO TO 200
C         CHECK FOR SPECIAL CASES OF MULTIPLE DEGREES OF FREEDOM
      150 CONTINUE
          DO 160 I=1,IDIM
          B=ABSF(BRTOT(I)-1.0)
          IF(B-1.0) 198,160,198
      160 CONTINUE
          DO 170 J=1,JDIM
          B=ABSF(BCTOT(J)-1.0)
          IF(B-1.0) 198,170,198
      170 CONTINUE
          KEY=3
          GO TO 200
      198 KEY=4
C         KEY=4 MEANS MORE THAN ONE DEGREE OF FREEDOM REMAINS, WITH COMPATIBILITY
      200 RETURN
          END

          SUBROUTINE SINDF(TABLE,TEMP2,ROWTOT,COLTOT,BTEMP,BRTOT,BCTOT,
         1BTOT,IDIM,JDIM)
C         THIS SUBROUTINE MAXIMIZES THE INDEX OF DISSIMILARITY WHEN ONLY
C         MULTIPLE SINGLE DEGREES OF FREEDOM REMAIN
          COMMON TABLE,BLOCK,BTEMP,TEMP1,TEMP2,ROWTOT,COLTOT,BRTOT,BCTOT,
         1BTOT,IDIM,JDIM,KEY,NEW,HOLD
          DIMENSION TABLE(17,17),BLOCK(17,17),BTEMP(17,17),TEMP1(17,17)
          DIMENSION TEMP2(17,17),ROWTOT(17),COLTOT(17),BRTOT(17),BCTOT(17)
          DIMENSION PARITY(17,17)
          DIMENSION HOLD(17,17)
          NBTOT=XFIXF(BTOT)
        1 DO 5 I=1,IDIM
          DO 5 J=1,JDIM
        5 PARITY(I,J)=0.0
C         FIRST HANDLE ANY ROWS WITH MORE THAN TWO CONSTRAINED CELLS
          DO 15 I=1,IDIM
          IF(BRTOT(I)-2.0) 15,15,20
       15 CONTINUE
          GO TO 160
       20 DO 25 J=1,JDIM
          IF(BTEMP(I,J)) 25,25,30
       25 CONTINUE
       30 PARITY(I,J)=1.0
          BTEMP(I,J)=0.0
          BRTOT(I)=BRTOT(I)-2.0
          MM=1
          IS=I
       64 DO 68 I=1,IDIM
          IF(BTEMP(I,J)) 68,68,70
       68 CONTINUE
```

175

```
   70 PARITY(I,J)=-1.0
      BTEMP(I,J)=0.0
      MM=MM+1
      IF(IS-I) 72,350,72
   72 DO 88 J=1,JDIM
      IF(BTEMP(I,J)) 88,88,90
   88 CONTINUE
   90 PARITY(I,J)=1.0
      BTEMP(I,J)=0.0
      BRTOT(I)=BRTOT(I)-2.0
      MM=MM+1
      GO TO 64
  160 DO 161 I=1,IDIM
      DO 161 J=1,JDIM
      IF(BTEMP(I,J)) 161,161,162
  161 CONTINUE
  162 PARITY(I,J)=1.0
      BTEMP(I,J)=0.0
      MM=1
      JS=J
  164 DO 168 J=1,JDIM
      IF(BTEMP(I,J)) 168,168,170
  168 CONTINUE
  170 PARITY(I,J)=-1.0
      BTEMP(I,J)=0.0
      MM=MM+1
      IF(JS-J) 172,350,172
  172 DO 188 I=1,IDIM
      IF(BTEMP(I,J)) 188,188,190
  188 CONTINUE
  190 PARITY(I,J)=1.0
      BTEMP(I,J)=0.0
      MM=MM+1
      GO TO 164
  350 DELTOP=0.0
      DO 390 II=1,IDIM
      DO 390 JJ=1,JDIM
      IF(PARITY(II,JJ)) 352,390,352
  352 I=II
      J=JJ
      TEMP2(I,J)=0.0
      S=TEMP2(I,J)
      CODE=PARITY(I,J)
      DEL=TABLE(I,J)
      M=1
  355 DO 365 J=1,JDIM
      IF(CODE+PARITY(I,J)) 365,360,365
  360 TEMP2(I,J)=ROWTOT(I)-S
      S=TEMP2(I,J)
      IF(S) 390,363,363
  363 CODE=PARITY(I,J)
      DEL=DEL+ABSF(TEMP2(I,J)-TABLE(I,J))
      M=M+1
      IF(M-MM) 366,385,385
  365 CONTINUE
  366 DO 375 I=1,IDIM
      IF(CODE+PARITY(I,J)) 375,370,375
  370 TEMP2(I,J)=COLTOT(J)-S
      S=TEMP2(I,J)
      IF(S) 390,373,373
  373 CODE=PARITY(I,J)
      DEL=DEL+ABSF(TEMP2(I,J)-TABLE(I,J))
      M=M+1
      IF(M-MM) 355,355,385
  375 CONTINUE
  385 IF(DEL-DELTOP) 390,390,388
  388 DELTOP=DEL
```

```
      DO 389 I=1,IDIM
      DO 389 J=1,JDIM
  389 TEMP1(I,J)=TEMP2(I,J)
  390 CONTINUE
  200 NBTOT=NBTOT-MM
      IF(NBTOT) 205,205,1
  205 DO 210 I=1,IDIM
      DO 210 J=1,JDIM
  210 TEMP2(I,J)=TEMP1(I,J)
      RETURN
      END

      SUBROUTINE COMP(TABLE,BLOCK,TEMP2,IDIM,JDIM)
C     THIS SUBROUTINE COMPUTES THE INDEX OF DISSIMILARITY BETWEEN TWO
C     TABLES, WRITES THE TABLE AND THE INDEX
      COMMON TABLE,BLOCK,BTEMP,TEMP1,TEMP2,ROWTOT,COLTOT,BRTOT,BCTOT,
     1BTOT,IDIM,JDIM,KEY,NEW,HOLD
      DIMENSION TABLE(17,17),BLOCK(17,17),BTEMP(17,17),TEMP1(17,17)
      DIMENSION TEMP2(17,17),ROWTOT(17),COLTOT(17),BRTOT(17),BCTOT(17)
      DIMENSION HOLD(17,17)
 3000 FORMAT(10X,40HMAXIMIN COEFFICIENT OF DISSIMILARITY IS , F10.6,//)
      TOTAL=0.0
      SUM=0.0
      DO 220 I=1,IDIM
      DO 220 J=1,JDIM
      IF(BLOCK(I,J)) 220,220,215
  215 TOTAL=TOTAL+TEMP2(I,J)
      SUM=SUM+ABSF(TABLE(I,J)-TEMP2(I,J))
  220 CONTINUE
      DELMAX=SUM/(2.0*TOTAL)
  222 WOT 6,3000,DELMAX
      RETURN
      END

      SUBROUTINE WRITE2(IDIM,JDIM,T)
C     THIS SUBROUTINE WRITES A TABLE WITH TOTALS COMPUTED WITHIN SUBROUTINE
      COMMON TABLE,BLOCK,BTEMP,TEMP1,TEMP2,ROWTOT,COLTOT,BRTOT,BCTOT,
     1BTOT,IDIM,JDIM,KEY,NEW,HOLD
      DIMENSION TABLE(17,17),BLOCK(17,17),BTEMP(17,17),TEMP1(17,17)
      DIMENSION TEMP2(17,17),ROWTOT(17),COLTOT(17),BRTOT(17),BCTOT(17)
      DIMENSION ROW(17),COL(17),T(17,17),NOCOL(17)
      DIMENSION HOLD(17,17)

 1000 FORMAT ( 1X,
     1        10HROW TOTALS,12X,9(2X,7HCOL NO.,I3),/,24X,9(9X,I3),//)
  110 FORMAT (F11.4,2X,7HROW NO.,I3,9F12.4,/,23X,9F12.4)
  120 FORMAT(/,F11.4,2X,10HCOL TOTALS,9F12.4,/,23X,9F12.4,///)
  130 FORMAT (/)
      DO 15 I=1,IDIM
   15 ROW(I)=0.0
      DO 20 J=1,JDIM
   20 COL(J)=0.0
      DO 25 I=1,IDIM
      DO 25 J=1,JDIM
      ROW(I)=ROW(I)+T(I,J)
   25 COL(J)=COL(J)+T(I,J)
      TOTAL=0.0
      DO 32 I=1,IDIM
   32 TOTAL=TOTAL+ROW(I)
      DO 5 J=1,JDIM
    5 NOCOL(J)=J
      WOT 6,100,(NOCOL(J),J=1,JDIM)
      WOT 6,130
      DO 10 I=1,IDIM
      WOT 6,110,ROW(I),I,(T(I,J),J=1,JDIM)
   10 WOT 6,130
      WOT 6,120,TOTAL,(COL(J),J=1,JDIM)
      WOT 6,130
      RETURN
      END
```

177

Bibliography

Bartholomew, D.J. (1967). Stochastic Models for Social Processes. New York: Wiley and Sons.

Beshers, J.M. and Laumann, E.O. (1967). "Social Distance: A Network Approach", American Sociological Review 32, 225–36.

Blau, P.M. and Duncan, O.D. (1967). The American Occupational Structure. New York: Wiley and Sons.

Blumen, I., Kogan, M. and McCarthy, P.J. (1955). The Industrial Mobility of Labor as a Probability Process. Cornell Studies of Industrial and Labor Relations, Vol. 8. Ithaca, New York: Cornell University Press.

Brownlee, K.A. (1965). Statistical Theory and Methodology in Science and Engineering. 2nd Ed. New York: Wiley and Sons.

Carlsson, G. (1958). Social Mobility and Class Structure. Lund, Sweden: W.K. Gleerup.

Connor, T.L. (1969). "A Stochastic Model for Occupations". Michigan State University: Unpublished paper.

Costner, H.L. (1965). "Criteria for Measures of Association", American Sociological Review 30, 341–53.

Deming, W.E. (1943). The Statistical Adjustment of Data. New York: Dover Books.

Duncan, O.D. (1966). "Methodological Issues in the Analysis of Social Mobility", in Smelser, N.J. and Lipset, S.M., eds. Social Structure and Mobility in Economic Development. Chicago: Aldine.

Duncan, O.D. and Duncan, B. (1955). "A Methodological Analysis of Segregation Indexes", American Sociological Review 20, 210–17.

Fiacco, A.V. and McCormick, G.P. (1968) Nonlinear Programming: Sequential Unconstrained Minimization Techniques. New York: Wiley and Sons.

Fienberg, S.E. (1969). "Preliminary Graphical Analysis and Quasi-Independence for Two-way Contingency Tables", The Journal of the Royal Statistical Society, Series B 18, 153–68.

Fienberg, S.E. (1970a). "An Iterative Procedure for Estimation in Contingency Tables", Annals of Mathematical Statistics 41, 907–17.

Fienberg, S.E. (1970b). "Quasi-Independence and Maximum Likelihood Estimation in Incomplete Contingency Tables", Journal of the American Statistical Association 65, 1610—1616.

Geiger, T. (1951). "Soziale Umschichtungen in einer Dänischen Mittelstadt", Acta Jutlandica 23, 340—60.

Glass, D.V., ed. (1954). Social Mobility in Britain. Glencoe, Illinois: Free Press.

Goodman, L.A. (1961). "Statistical Methods for the Mover-Stayer Model", Journal of the American Statistical Assocation 56, 841—68.

Goodman, L.A. (1965). "On the Statistical Analysis of Mobility Tables", American Journal of Sociology 70, 564—85.

Goodman, L.A. (1967). "On the Reconciliation of the Mathematical Theories of Population Growth", Journal of the Royal Statistical Society, Series A 130, 541—54.

Goodman, L.A. (1968a). "The Analysis of Cross-Classified Data: Independence, Quasi-Independence, and Interactions in Contingency Tables with or without Missing Entries", Journal of the American Statistical Association 63, 1091—1131.

Goodman, L.A. (1968b). "Stochastic Models for the Population Growth of the Sexes", Biometrika 55, 469—87.

Goodman, L.A. (1969a). "The Analysis of Population Growth When the Birth and Death Rates Depend Upon Several Factors", Biometrics 25, 659—81.

Goodman, L.A. (1969b). "How to Ransack Social Mobility Tables and Other Kinds of Cross-Classification Tables", American Journal of Sociology 75, 1—40.

Goodman, L.A. (1969c). "On the Measurement of Social Mobility: An Index of Status Persistence", American Sociological Review 34, 831—50.

Goodman, L.A. (1970). "Mathematical Models and Statistical Methods for the Analysis of Mobility Tables and Other Kinds of Cross-Classification Tables", University of Chicago: Mimeographed.

Goodman, Leo A. (1971a). "The Analysis of Multidimensional Contingency Tables: Stepwise Procedures and Direct Estimation Methods for Building Models for Multiple Classifications", Technometrics 13, 33—61.

Goodman, L.A. (1971b). "Some Multiplicative Models for the Analysis of Cross-Classified Data", Proceedings, Sixth Berkeley Symposium on Mathematical Statistics and Probability. Berkeley: University of California Press, 649—696.

Goodman, L.A. and Kruskal, W.H. (1954). "Measures of Association", Journal of the American Statistical Assocation 49, 732—64.

Goodman, L.A. and Kruskal, W.H. (1963). "Measures of Association for Cross-classifications III: Approximate Sampling Theory", Journal of the American Statistical Association 58, 310—64.

Haberman, S. (1974). "The Analysis of Frequency Data". Chicago: University of Chicago Press.

Harris, T.E. (1951). "Some Mathematical Models for Branching Processes", in Proceedings, Second Berkeley Symposium on Mathematical Statistics and Probability, pp. 305—28. Berkeley: University of California Press.

Harris, T.E. (1963). The Theory of Branching Processes. Berlin: Springer-Verlag.

Hodge, R.W. (1966). "Occupational Mobility as a Probability Process", Demography 3, 19–34.

Hope, K. (1971). "Social Mobility and Fertility", American Sociological Review 36, 1019–32.

Hutchinson, B. (1958). "Structural and Exchange Mobility in the Assimilation of Immigrants to Brazil", Population Studies 12, 111–20.

Johnson, N.L. and Kotz, S. (1969). Discrete Distributions. Boston: Houghton Mifflin Co.

Kahl, J.A. (1957). The American Class Structure. New York: Rinehart.

Karlin, S. (1968). A First Course in Stochastic Processes. New York: Academic Press.

Kemeny, J.G. and Snell, J.L. (1960). Finite Markov Chains. Princeton, New Jersey: D. Van Nostrand.

Keyfitz, N. (1968). Introduction to the Mathematics of Population. Reading, Mass.: Addison-Wesley.

Keyfitz, N. (1973). "Individual Mobility in a Stationary Population", Population Studies 27, 335–52.

Lazarsfeld, P.F. and Henry, N.W. (1966). Readings in Mathematical Social Sciences. Chicago: Science Research Associates.

Levine, J.H. (1967). "Measurement in the Study of Inter-Generational Status Mobility". Harvard University: Unpublished Ph.D. Dissertation.

Levine, J.H. (1969). "Decay Analysis of a Coefficient of Labor Immobility". University of Michigan: Unpublished paper.

Lipset, S.M. and Bandix, R. (1964). Social Mobility in Industrial Society. Berkeley: University of California Press.

Mantel, N. (1970). "Incomplete Contingency Tables", Biometrics 26, 291–304.

Matras, J. (1960). "Comparison of Inter-Generational Occupational Mobility Patterns", Population Studies 14, 163–69.

Matras, J. (1961). "Differential Fertility, Inter-Generational Mobility and Change in the Occupational Structure," Population Studies 15, 187–97.

Matras, J. (1967). "Social Mobility and Social Structure: Some Insights from the Linear Model", American Sociological Review 32, 608–14.

Mayer, T.F. (1967). "Birth and Death Process Models of Social Mobility", Michigan Studies in Mathematical Sociology, No. 2, University of Michigan.

Mayer, T.F. (1968). "Age and Mobility: Two Approaches to the Problem of Non-Stationarity", Michigan Studies in Mathematical Sociology, No. 6, University of Michigan.

McFarland, D.D. (1968). "An Extension of Conjoint Measurement to Test the Theory of Quasi-Perfect Mobility", Michigan Studies in Mathematical Sociology, No. 3, University of Michigan.

McFarland, D.D. (1969a). "Measuring the Permeability of Occupational Structures", American Journal of Sociology 75, 41–61.

McFarland, D.D. (1969b). "Social Distance as a Metric". University of Michigan: Unpublished paper.

McFarland, D.D. (1970). "Intra-Generational Social Mobility as a Markov Process: Including a Time-Stationary Markovian Model that Explains Observed Declines in Mobility Rates Over Time", American Sociological Review 35, 463–76.

McFarland, D.D. and Brown, D.J. (1971). "Social Distance: Foundations and Procedures", in Laumann, E.O., ed., Informal Networks and Value Orientations in a Metropolis. Chicago: Markham Press.

McGinnis, R. (1968). "A Stochastic Model of Social Mobility", American Sociological Review 33, 712–22.

Miller, S.M. (1960). "Comparative Social Mobility", Current Sociology 9, 1–89.

Morrison, P.A. (1967). "Duration of Residence and Prospective Migration: The Evaluation of a Stochastic Model", Demography 4, 553–61.

Mosteller, F. (1968). "Association and Estimation in Contingency Tables", Journal of the American Statistical Association 63, 1–28.

Nishira, S. (1957). "Cross-National Comparative Study on Social Stratification and Social Mobility", Annals of the Institute of Statistical Mathematics 8, 181–91.

Palmer, G.L. (1954). Labor Mobility in Six Cities. New York: Social Science Research Council.

Pollard, J.H. (1966). "On the Use of the Direct Matrix Product in Analyzing Certain Stochastic Population Models", Biometrika 53, 397–415.

Prais, S.J. (1955). "The Formal Theory of Social Mobility", Population Studies 9, 72–81.

Pullum, T.W. (1964). "The Theoretical Implications of Quasi-Perfect Mobility". The University of Chicago: Unpublished paper.

Pullum, T.W. (1968). "Occupational Mobility as a Branching Process". Department of Statistics, The University of Chicago: Unpublished S.M. paper.

Rogers, Andrei (1968). Matrix Analysis of Inter-regional Population Growth and Distribution. Berkeley: University of California Press.

Rogoff, N. (1953). Recent Trends in Occupational Mobility. Glencoe, Ill.: Free Press.

Sibley, E. (1942). "Some Demographic Clues to Stratification", American Sociological Review 8, 322–30.

Simon, H.A. (1957). Models of Man. New York: Wiley and Sons.

Sovani, N.V. and Pradhan, K. (1955). "Occupational Mobility in Poona City between Three Generations", Indian Economic Review 2, 23–36.

Spilerman, S. (1972). "Extensions of the Mover-Stayer Model". American Journal of Sociology 78, 599–626.

Svalastoga, K. (1959). Prestige, Class and Mobility. Copenhagen: Gyldendal.

Theil, H. and Finizza, A.J. (1971). "A Note on the Measurement of Racial Integration of Schools by means of Informational Concepts", Journal of Mathematical Sociology 1, 187–193.

Treiman, D. (1968). "Occupational Prestige and Social Structure: A Cross-National Comparison". The University of Chicago: Unpublished Ph.D. dissertation.

Tumin, M.M. and Feldman, A.S. (1961). Social Class and Social Change in Puerto Rico. Princeton, New Jersey: Princeton University Press.

Tyree, A. (1973). "Mobility Ratios and Association in Mobility Tables", Population Studies 27, 577–88.

Wagner, S.S. (1970). "The Maximum-Likelihood Estimate for Contingency Tables with Zero Diagonal", Journal of the American Statistical Association 65, 1362–83.

White, H.C. (1963). "Cause and Effect in Social Mobility Tables", Behavioral Science 8, 14–27.

White, H.C. (1970). Chains of Opportunity: System Models of Mobility in Organizations. Cambridge, Mass.: Harvard University Press.

Wiley, J. (1966). "Inter-Generational Status Mobility: Some Tests of Goodman's Model". Washington University, St. Louis: Unpublished paper.

Index